DECODING COLLEGE

STORIES, STRATEGIES, AND STRUGGLES OF FIRST-GENERATION COLLEGE STUDENTS

KALLIE CLARK

Rowe Publishing

Copyright © 2017 by Kallie Clark.
All rights reserved.

ISBN 13: 978-1-939054-76-0
ISBN 10: 1-939054-76-1

No portion of this work may be used or reproduced in any manner whatsoever without written permission, except in the case of brief quotations embodied in articles and reviews.

To protect the privacy of those involved, names, locations, and/or dates have been changed, and composite characters were created when necessary.

Statements and opinions expressed by the author are not necessarily those of the publisher and its affiliates. Neither shall be liable for erroneous information.

1 3 5 7 9 8 6 4 2

Printed in the United States of America
Published by

Rowe Publishing
www.rowepub.com

To the students who were brave enough
to share their stories:
I hear you.

For Marcella:
My everything.

A special thank you to
Mom, Denisse, Clover, and Maxine.

Contents

Preface: Why I Wrote This Book 1
Introduction: Is College for You? 5

SECTION 1: Finding the Right College 9
Chapter 1: It's Not You, It's Them 11
    Recognize the Red Flags 15
    Elena: For-Profit Sinkhole 19
    There Are No Easy Answers 20
    Break It Down: Elena 21
    Recognize the Good Ones 22
Chapter 2: Cultivating Your Inner Ninja 26
    Lucas: A College Success Story 26
    It's What's On the Inside that Counts 31
    Break It Down: Lucas 33
Chapter 3: Your College Application Strategy 34
Chapter 4: Strategy Glossary 37
Chapter 5: Using Your College Application Strategy . . . 67
Chapter 6: Finding Colleges for Your Strategy 68
Chapter 7: College Lists 72
Chapter 8: Fit Is Flavor 86
    Malik: It Just Didn't Click 86
    Success Is a Two-Way Street 91
    Break It Down: Malik 93
Chapter 9: You Are More Than a Number 94
    Jasmine: Put Yourself Out There 95
    A Case for Playing the Field 98
    Break It Down: Jasmine 102

SECTION 2: Succeeding in College 105
Introduction 107

Chapter 10: The Many Colors of Racism 108
    Aubrey: Expected to Fail 108
    Race, Power, and Privilege 112
    Break It Down: Aubrey. 115
    Dominique: The Importance of Family. 116
    An Extended Family .120
    Break It Down: Dominique 122
Chapter 11: Working Hard or Hardly Working 123
    Isabel: No Room for Failure 124
    Making the Most Of It 127
    Break It Down: Isabel. 128
    Eric: Hard Today, Harder Tomorrow 129
    The Only Way to Go Is Up 133
    Break It Down: Eric. .135
Chapter 12: Belonging 136
    Emmy: Culture Shock 137
    To Thine own Self Be True. 140
    Break It Down: Emmy 141
    Sophia: All I Have Ever Wanted 142
    Winning a Rigged Game 147
    Break It Down: Sophia 148
    The Art of Graduating 149

SECTION 3: College Knowledge 151
Chapter 13: Tips, Tricks, and Tools. 153
    Before You Apply 154
    Preparing to Apply 154
    Presenting Yourself as a Candidate 159
    Paying for College. 171
    Applying 177
    Decision Time. 183

PREFACE

Why I Wrote This Book

I was raised believing that college was for "those" kids: the ones with the right shoes, the right clothes, and the right social status. My mother did everything in her power to ensure we got the best education possible in the public school system, but when it came to college I was on my own. College representatives would visit my high school and pass around shiny pamphlets filled with images of beautiful buildings and beautiful people, but every time the discussion of tuition came up I would tune out. The idea that this magical thing called financial aid was going to somehow make a $30,000 a year college affordable was ludicrous to me. The topic of college remained something I avoided, up until the spring of my senior year.

On an otherwise uneventful day my AP English teacher, Ms. Rose, did something that finally made me confront my assumptions about college. As I shuffled into her class I spotted a carefully crafted list on the white board at the front of the room. The first column had each of our names listed alphabetically. The second column was blank except for a single word at the top: college. Slowly as the weeks ticked by that board began to fill up. It seemed like every student in the entire school had a college next to their name but me. It was May of my senior year, and I had missed the application deadlines for most colleges. I was lost, embarrassed, and scared about what my life would look like after high school. One of my closest friends asked her mother what I should do. She insisted that I needed to go to college and told me about a local state university that might still be accepting applications. I walked my application and transcript into the admissions office, sat down, and waited to hear why I wouldn't be accepted. But I was accepted. I was admitted on the spot. I was going to college.

My mother was proud. My grandmother was actually so impressed she whistled when I told her I was going to a four-year university. I had no idea that I could have done more. As I watched my closest friends go off to Berkeley and Wellesley I began to understand that colleges aren't all the same. I worked full-time at coffee shops to pay my way through school, but life was hard. I was often not able to stay on top of my bills, and there were some days when the only food I ate was the free meal I was allowed during my shift at work—but I trekked on. As my friends graduated four years later, I was still nowhere near graduating. Working full-time had left me exhausted. By the time I completed my bachelor's degree I finally understood what I had missed out on so many years before. I wanted to go back in time and apply to every one of those colleges that looked so magical to me as a senior. I wanted a do-over, but of course there would be no do-over. Instead, I picked myself up and marched on.

Some years later, I moved to Chicago and earned my master's degree. After graduating I began teaching at a local high school. Over the years I moved up in position and eventually became the school's college counselor. I realized that I was really good at problem solving with my students. I felt comfortable being candid with them in ways that many people weren't. I did my absolute best to ensure than no one fell through the cracks—that no one would be in the same boat that I was in back in high school. After several years I knew that I wanted to have an impact beyond the walls of my classroom.

I went back to school (some ten years older than my peers) and earned a master's from The University of Chicago's School of Social Service Administration. I blossomed and grew beyond measure. The level of support I received was astounding. The professors were invested in my growth and development in ways I never imagined. I felt nurtured for the first time as a student. I gained courage in my abilities, and developed the skills I needed to ultimately be accepted into the doctorate program at SSA. It took me twenty years to finally experience what my friends were able to experience right out of high school. While my road has not been the quickest, or the straightest, it sure has been one heck of a journey.

I am not here to tell you that I have all the answers, or that the road through college (or life for that matter) is going to be easy. In fact, it probably won't be easy. But, I can tell you that earning your college degree is worth every single bump and bruise you endure along the way. I can also offer you this book: a small and mighty collection of resources to help you navigate the college application process and avoid some of the most treacherous pitfalls on your own journey through higher education. When you feel alone or confused, remember you are widening the path to college for those that follow you—for your brothers and sisters, cousins, children, and countless strangers you will never meet. Every step you take leaves footprints on the trail to guide others. You don't need to be perfect. Your path doesn't need to be the quickest or the straightest. Just focus on the road ahead. Take one step at a time. And in the words of a former student of mine, *learn to love the struggle*, for it will lead you to a beautiful place.

Introduction

Is College For You?

Deciding whether or not you should go to college might feel like a difficult decision, but actually of all the decisions to be made in the college process, this one—I think—is the simplest. If you are asking yourself "Is college right for me?," the answer is very short, and very definitive: yes. Yes, college is for you. College comes in a wide variety of shapes and sizes: everything from a traditional four-year degree to earning a certificate in a technical trade. There is a place for you in college if you want it. The real question is do you want it? And if you don't, what's your alternative plan?

There are two types of students who are sure they do not want to go to college: those that have a solid plan after high school, and those that don't. Students who have a solid plan that does not include college are not necessarily choosing the easy way out. More often than not, these plans include an immense amount of work and dedication in order to reach a very tangible goal, like enrolling in the military. Simply saying that you are going to enroll in the military is not the same thing as having a solid plan. Having a solid plan includes steps like meeting with military recruiters, researching positions within the different branches of the military, understanding the different exam scores required for the positions you are interested in, taking practice exams, and fitting in study time to raise your exam score if necessary. These students are not leaving their future to wishful thinking; they have made a plan and are actively pursuing it.

Students who choose not to go to college, and don't have a plan are—more often than not—just sick of school. This is so unfortunate, because they are making a long-term decision based on a temporary feeling. You are not going to be in school forever. Whether you leave school now or a few years from now, one day you will have your last class, and for the rest of your life you will be in the workforce. Think high school is a pain? Try working in the service industry for thirty years. You can't avoid work. College is work. Not going to college is work. Life is work. Work isn't going away any time soon. If you quit trying to avoid work and start thinking about what you want the rest of your life to look like you will have a much easier time deciding what you really want to do after high school. Every student—regardless of academic ability—should actively decide if college is right for them. It is important that you take responsibility for *choosing* college or *not choosing* college and the immense amount of work that comes along with either decision.

A much more difficult question is what kind of college is right for you. This really boils down to whether you want a certificate, a two-year degree (associate's), or a four-year degree (bachelor's). Obviously, some degrees take longer to earn than other degrees. But, beyond that, each type of degree serves a different purpose. A certificate represents training to learn a limited set of skills within a specific trade. Certificate programs can range from air conditioning and refrigeration repair to pharmaceutical science. It is important to be familiar with the potential career opportunities and limitations with getting a certificate. A certificate in air conditioning and refrigeration might qualify you to work as a service technician, but it might not qualify you to manage the service department. Likewise, a certificate in pharmaceutical science might qualify you to work as a pharmacy technician, but it won't provide the same career (or salary) opportunities as being a pharmacist. Associate's degrees are two-year degrees that have general education coursework and coursework within a specific area. Associate's degrees can offer more opportunities for career advancement than certificates, and do not take much longer to earn. A bachelor's degree takes longer to earn than an associate's degree; however, it offers the greatest opportunity for career advancement and potential earnings. With a bachelor's degree you can enter into the workforce or pursue an advanced degree such as a master's or a doctorate.

If you were/are a strong student I would argue that a four-year degree is your best bet. The payoff for earning a bachelor's degree is usually much greater than earning an associate's degree or certificate, and it doesn't require much more time. If you have struggled academically in high school you need to figure out why. Were you putting in your full effort and still barely able to keep your head above water? If so, you might want to consider starting at a two-year and transferring to a four year college later on, or earning an associate's degree. Were you capable of a lot more academically but just didn't put in the effort? Then I would argue that you should keep a four-year college on the table and see how the admissions decisions turn out. You might get into a four-year college as a freshman or you might need to start at a community college and get your academics together before you can transfer. Lastly, if you are the kind of student who struggles significantly in school and wants to get to work as soon as possible, then you might consider a certificate program.

If you are feeling pressure to make the "right" college decision, I want to take a moment and reassure you that things will sort themselves out with time. You don't need to have a solid college plan to read this book. In fact, this book was written specifically for students who don't have a solid college plan. As a former college counselor, I know that many public school students do not have access to comprehensive guidance in the college search process. As a first-generation college student, I know first-hand how mysterious and daunting the college search process can be. It's true, applying to college is going to take time and energy, but it's not rocket science either. Chances are you already have the skills you need to get into a good college; you just need to know the rules of the game. In the next few sections, I am going to lay out step-by-step what you need to do to develop a good college application list. In Section 3 we'll talk briefly about some of the more mysterious aspects of applying to colleges, such as essay writing and financial aid. By the end of our literary journey together, you should be in a pretty solid place to take on your college applications.

Before we get to the nitty-gritty about getting you into college, I think we should take a moment and talk about what that means exactly. If you are reading this book in hopes of learning exactly what you need to do to get into the college of your dreams, I will tell you right now I have no idea. In fact, no one does. Because the college of your dreams today might be different than the college of your dreams two years from now—or even tomorrow! Trying to get into the college of your dreams is a quest that is only going to set you up for failure. Instead, focus on getting into a college that is going to serve you well. If getting into a good quality college becomes your goal, you are much more likely to succeed and reap the benefits of that success.

You should consider a college a good quality college if it does these four things:

❶ Has a strong graduation rate;

❷ Will be financially sustainable;

❸ Will challenge you to grow academically and personally;

❹ Will provide the supports that you need to be academically and socially successful.

SECTION 1

FINDING THE RIGHT COLLEGE

Chapter 1

It's Not You, It's Them

The biggest lie students are told about college is that success is solely a reflection of their efforts and abilities. Sure, you probably aren't going to be very successful in college if you don't attend class or study regularly. But attending class and studying don't guarantee that you will do well in college. Why? You might be quick to point out that not all students are bright enough to handle college-level material or that not all students are ready for the demands of college-level work. While this could be the case sometimes, I would suggest that more often than not student failure is much more complicated than we have been led to believe. The model of college success that most students are presented with looks a lot like this:

$$\text{Effort} + \text{Ability} = \text{Success}$$

The version above is beautiful in it's simplicity. It makes sense. It feels right. You know from experience that when you work harder you tend to perform better. How can anyone argue against this? They can't, which is why the version above is so popular with colleges and high schools alike. But, I am going to point out an assumption that is often made—but rarely addressed—when people talk about success in college (and school in general). The default way people speak and think about college success is almost exclusively focused on the student, even though no one explicitly says so. When people talk about success being determined by effort and ability they are talking about a very one-sided version of effort and ability. What they really mean is something like this:

$$\text{Student's Effort} + \text{Student's Ability} = \text{Student's Success}$$

Okay, I'll admit that the version above is probably accurate to an extent; but I would also argue that it isn't entirely true. In fact, sometimes it is sadly not true at all. All the effort in the world won't get you very far if you happen to get caught up in the bureaucracy of a poorly run college. Yes, you have a responsibility to take college seriously and invest your fullest time and energy into doing well. But before you are admitted (and before you ever apply) you should be thinking about your college success from this perspective:

$$\text{College's Effort} + \text{College's Ability} = \text{College's Success}$$

Wait! What? What are a college's effort, ability, and success? It's quite simple. **A successful college is one that educates and graduates students in a timely manner.** We are so used to putting the burden of success on students that we forget students don't go to school in a vacuum. Where you go to school matters just as much as your abilities as a student. If you were shopping for a car you would look at how that car performs compared to other cars in your price range.

If a sales person presented you with a clunker of a car, you would quickly walk the other way. You wouldn't say, "I'm a great driver. I don't need to worry about car safety or reliability!" No. Because your ability to get from point A to point B is just as much about your ability to drive as it is about your car's ability to get you there safely and efficiently. In fact, if you weren't happy with the reliability of the options on the lower end of the price range, you might decide to take out a car loan to get into a more reliable car. Selecting a college is no different. We rarely talk about the college's effort in providing students with adequate resources or supports, or the college's ability to provide high quality instruction, and we almost never talk about the failure of the school to provide a quality education in a timely manner. You may not have had a lot of choice in where you went to school up to this point in your life, but that is all about to change. If you are going to be a savvy college consumer you need to approach selecting a college with as much scrutiny as you would when buying a car.

Colleges have a responsibility to do everything within reason to graduate the students they admit, and yet a lot of colleges don't. Colleges with low graduation rates bank on the fact that a new flood of freshmen will be their bread and butter the following year, thus continuing the endless cycle of students going to college and leaving college with debt and without a degree. Most colleges (even those colleges with low graduation rates) have good intentions. However, just because a college has good intentions doesn't mean they are doing a good job of identifying and meeting the needs of their students, and it certainly doesn't mean that you should pay the price for their poor performance.

Take the issue of college writing for example. It is common for college grades to be based entirely on two or three papers or exams. A poor performing college might have a writing center, but not do a very good job at connecting students to this service. In really great colleges you will find writing services interwoven into the freshman writing classes. This ensures that all students receive services proactively before they are struggling and better equips students to seek out resources if they do struggle. Inevitably, students will hit rocky patches in the first two years of college. How well a college acknowledges, addresses, and even anticipates these struggles directly affects how many of their students will make it through these rough patches and on to graduation.

It is true that different schools admit different types of students who have different needs and resources, but it is still the responsibility of the college to meet the needs of the students they are admitting. Remember, colleges pick their students. If they don't have faith in their own ability to graduate the students they admit, then why on earth are they taking their money?

Do you want to know if a college is doing a good job serving their students? Look at the college's graduation rate. If you are a student of color, also look at the school's minority student graduation rate. These things matter. If a car has a long history of breaking down, you can be pretty sure it is going to break down again whether you or someone else is driving it. Sure, cars can break down because of driver error, but a car with a track record of breaking down probably has some serious mechanical issues that you want no part of. Graduation rate is like the number of times a car has broken down in the last year. A college with a 20 percent graduation rate is like a car that breaks down 80 percent of the time. We can focus on the 20 percent of the time that it did run, or try and blame 80 percent of the drivers, but that is kind of silly. Unfortunately, there is no one number that represents a good graduation rate or a bad graduation rate. It all boils down to comparing the graduation rates of the colleges you have access to.

Without a doubt, you do need to do your part as a student. You need to work hard. You need to put your full effort into utilizing resources, studying, and managing your time to ensure you are performing to the best of your ability. But, it is not enough to only look inward. When evaluating potential colleges, look for evidence of their effort to provide you with a strong education in a timely manner. What is the college's graduation rate? What evidence is there that students are receiving a quality education? Sit in on a class. Is the material engaging? Is the professor organized, energetic, and able to connect with the students? Talk to current students. Are they happy with their choice to attend this school? Why did they select this college? Ask yourself if you want *their story* to be *your story* a few years from now. If not, what are you going to do differently?

Recognize the Red Flags

Perhaps you come to the college game with a good deal of advice and experience already. Or perhaps, like most of us, you come to the world of applying to college with very little in your toolbox. Either way, the following section will help you identify colleges that will do more harm than good, and how to pick out the ones that are genuinely "good catches."

Opportunistic Colleges

There is an established ritual for asking someone out that depends largely on location. At a party? Sure. At a funeral? No, definitely not. Why? Because it's predatory and takes advantage of the fact that you are emotionally vulnerable. The same goes with colleges. If a college is going to approach you about admissions it should be in a location that communicates mutual interest: a college campus, a college fair, or high school classroom. It shouldn't be at the local mall or on your television while you are in your PJs. Approaching you in these situations is a red flag that the college is looking for people who are down on their luck and vulnerable. Many students who are the first in their family to go to college get hustled into enrolling in college this way. Don't fall for it. Predatory colleges are counting on the fact that you are unfamiliar with college options, and they are taking advantage of that.

Your Money and Time Matter

As we have already discussed, graduation rates matter. Assuming that you are going to college to actually earn a degree, there is no better way to predict your chances of earning that degree than looking at a potential college's graduation rate. The temptation is to discount the importance of graduation rates and assume that you are going to have a different experience than the rest of your peers. The problem is that many academically capable and driven students drop out of college every day. Pure and simple, a school's graduation rate is a clear testament of that school's ability to graduate the students they admit.

The Bait and Switch

A lot of colleges will extend offers of scholarships with their admissions letters. The inclination can be to accept the school that offers you the largest scholarship. But be careful: that scholarship might be a bait and switch, meaning just because they offer you a nice scholarship initially doesn't mean that the school will be affordable, now or in the long run. A ten thousand dollar scholarship sounds really nice, but it means very little until you know how much the school is going to cost you per year. You won't know this until you get your financial aid award letter. Award letters are the official breakdown of costs from each school you were admitted to. Sometimes the school with the highest tuition will be your most affordable choice in the end. Sometimes the school that offers you the biggest scholarship on your acceptance letter won't be the most affordable once all your financial aid is calculated and costs are taken into consideration. These initial scholarships are meant to get your interest and get you to take the school's offer of admissions seriously, and you absolutely should. But don't get ahead of the game, unless of course you see the words "full tuition scholarship."

Money First, Students Last

When a school is a for-profit college you can take that as a sure sign that they are more interested in your money than your education. For-profit colleges are just that: out to make as much profit as possible. Admissions jobs at for-profit colleges often look a lot like sales jobs. Many are commission based, so there is an incentive to get you to purchase their education. To for-profit colleges you are primarily a customer buying a product, and they are eager to sell it to you. Whether that product is valuable or useful to you, or whether you actually ever receive it, is not their highest priority. These are buy-at-your-own-risk kind of colleges. There are certain times when such an institution might be useful (for instance if you already have a bachelor's degree and need an advanced degree to move up at work), but most likely these situations do not apply to you right now. Skip the for-profit colleges and save yourself a ton of heartache (and money).

Communication is Key

College admissions offices, counselors, and financial aid officers are *really* busy. And yes, it is reasonable to expect that you are going to have to carry the burden of initiating communication between the two of you. But, you should not be continuously ignored. While there are fantastic schools that do an amazing job of initiating communication with their potential students, this is not the case most of the time. However, if you are calling, emailing, and continuously unable to reach a helpful human, then you need to consider how attentive this college is going to be to your needs in the future. If they don't care about you now, chances are they won't care about you later.

You Never Had a Chance

It feels good to be wanted. It's flattering to get a letter or email encouraging you to apply to a specific college. You may even receive an offer to waive your application fee or a promise of a $3,000 scholarship without even knowing your GPA. While some of these gestures are opportunities from schools that are genuinely interested in you, some are going to be from schools that have no intention to admit you. Why? It makes perfect sense from the college's standpoint. Unless you are an open-enrollment college (like a community college), you want as many people to apply to your school as possible.

Consider a college that has 400 slots for incoming freshmen, and only receives 500 applications. This school has an acceptance rate of 80 percent, which is really high. A really high acceptance rate is like saying "we'll take anyone." It's kind of a turn-off to potential students. However, if the same college can boost the number of students applying to 1000, they have reduced their acceptance rate to 40 percent. This makes the school look more prestigious and more appealing, thus drawing in students with higher qualifications. In this formula, the prestige of the school is artificially inflated, and it doesn't matter whether those additional 500 students all had 2.0s; the result is the same.

The only way to avoid wasting your time applying to schools that you don't have a chance with is to do your research. Only apply to schools that you know the admissions data for. What is the range of SAT/ACT and GPA for admitted students? If the school has a middle GPA range of 3.2-3.6 and middle ACT range of 23-27, and you have a GPA of 2.5 and an ACT of 16, then you should be highly suspicious that they are using you to boost their numbers. It's okay to be a little under the average if you can offer a unique set of talents, skills, or life experiences that can increase campus diversity. But if you are way under, you might want to invest your time in a more serious prospect.

ELENA

For-Profit Sinkhole

I was going to go away to college, but I went through a really bad domestic violence experience, and I decided to stay at home. I took a year off, and then I knew I wanted to go to college. My brother told me about Focal Point College, this for-profit college, and I ended up listening to him. I didn't research it for myself, and it was horrible. I'm $10,000 in debt and I was only there a year! I am paying my loan off right now, but I am paying more on my interest than on my actual loan. To be honest, I don't even know if I can afford to go back to school because of the student loans I got at Focal Point. My brother went to Focal Point too. He finally has his bachelor's, but it cost him like $60,000. After he graduated, he applied for jobs but didn't get any interviews. He would apply, but he didn't know how to interview. And he kept going back to the school and asking if they could help him with his resume, or with getting a job, but they wouldn't help him. So, he had to do it on his own. He just recently got hired, but I think he got lucky.

Focal Point College is more like a sales business. You go in and, you know, they give you these numbers. I just did it because my brother said it was good, and I shouldn't have gone there. I should have started someplace else. I don't really remember how I signed up. You know how when you go to buy a car, that's how it was. That's exactly how it was. They were like, "Oh, come on. You should do this, do that. It's hard to explain, but it was like I went to a dealership, and they were trying to sell me something.

After I signed up I went for like a week at one campus, but it was too far, and so I went to the downtown campus. I remember it was terrible. They only had one advisor, and they didn't have a financial aid office at all. I remember trying to understand my financial aid, and they only had the one advisor. She had all these students waiting to see her. Then she stuck me in this Computer 101 class, and I refused to take it. She stuck me in the same class three times, and I kept telling her I didn't want to take it. It wasn't until after Focal Point had academically dismissed me that I found out I had other class options that I could have taken online. I could have saved money and taken the class I wanted to take, but she never even told me that. She never gave me any other option.

There Are No Easy Answers

There is a reason why Elena's story is the first student story presented in this book: what Elena experienced is so incredibly common for first-generation college students. Elena is a perfect example of why the college you choose to attend matters. Simply put, the college Elena chose to attend failed to provide the quality education and services she needed to earn a degree in a timely manner. The school's abysmal graduation rate is evidence of such. It is also clear that the school did not have Elena's best interests in mind. If they did, they never would have registered her for courses that she didn't need, didn't want to take, and couldn't afford to take in the first place. $10,000 for one year of college might be a good deal if you are going to a top-tier school with a top-notch graduation rate and reputation. But, paying $10,000 a year to a school that can't even graduate its students is ridiculous. So is paying $60,000 for a degree that can't even land you a job interview.

It's upsetting to know that Elena had such a negative experience with college and I can't help but feel like this school took advantage of her. At the same time, it is totally understandable how Elena ended up in the spot she is in. For-profit colleges are actively seeking out people just like Elena—people who want a better future, but have limited resources to get there. Elena was definitely academically capable of being successful in college, but she faced some very serious circumstances in her life that made the transition to college difficult. In our interview Elena mentioned that there was still a part of her that wished she had gone away to school, but she also acknowledged the devastating effects of being a survivor of domestic violence. Abuse and trauma can be emotionally, physically, and spiritually devastating. Elena did everything she could to take care of herself and get her life on the right track, and I am so proud of her. It's been several years since Elena's experience with Focal Point, and she now has a supportive husband and beautiful young children. But, she also has $10,000 in debt and not a single college course to show for it.

Elena's experience illustrates that there are no easy answers. Running off to college isn't going to solve all of your problems. Neither is staying home. You have to look the future head on and make the best choices you can. Not every college is the answer to our problems. Colleges can be an avenue to economic stability and opportunity, but only if we are careful and choose wisely.

BREAK IT DOWN

Elena

- What advice do you think you would have given Elena back in high school?
- What advice would you give her now?
- Do you think her college was worth $10,000 a year?
- Do you think any college is worth $10,000 a year? Why or why not?

Recognize the Good Ones

They Put You First

Probably the greatest sign that a college is a keeper is if they place you and your future before their numbers. This is usually evident pretty early on in how the school communicates with potential students. Admissions officers who are open, honest, and interested in helping you find the right college for you (even if it is not their school) most likely represent colleges who will be equally supportive of you once you are on campus. If you want to major in nursing, and the admissions representative is trying to sell you on the benefits of majoring in biology, without mentioning the potential limitations of such a choice, you might want to take that as a warning sign that the school is more interested in enrolling you than helping you meet your future goals. However, if the admissions rep acknowledges your desire to go into nursing, discusses the possibility of a joint degree with another institution, discusses the benefits and limitations of being pre-med instead, or is honest enough to tell you that you might be better off attending another institution, these are all signs that the rep is listening and trying to find a way to support you in your future goals.

They Have Nothing to Hide

A school that connects you to students and faculty who can share their honest opinions and experiences is definitely starting off on the right foot. Chances are if current and former students have had good experiences, you will too. If you have the opportunity to speak to students with similar interests, goals, or background as you, this can be especially helpful. These students can offer you insight into obstacles and supports you couldn't even imagine at this point in your academic career. Being connected early to faculty is also a sign of a keeper college. Attentive faculty in the college admissions process indicates that the school has a culture of academic investment in their students, and more than likely work to actively cultivate supportive relationships between faculty and students. Having a faculty member in your corner to mentor you, offer advice, or even just offer encouragement can be the difference between excelling in college and struggling to make it in college. If you are offered the opportunity to connect with a faculty member, do it!

They are a Straight Shooter

Most schools won't give you a minimum standardized test-score or GPA that you need for admissions. Even most elite colleges will tell you that they don't have minimum criteria for admissions and will proudly boast that they have a holistic review process. In reality, unless you bring something exceptional to the table (or happen to be the offspring of someone exceptional), there are academic standards which institutions strive to maintain. While a college probably won't come right out and tell you what these are, a good institution will be upfront and comfortable guiding you in ways that allow you to present yourself as a stronger applicant. Admissions shouldn't be a mystery. A good college admissions rep will advise you on whether you should focus on raising your standardized test scores, highlighting your unique life experiences, or focus on taking the most rigorous courses available at your high school (or all of the above).

In instances where your likelihood of being admitted is very low, a good college will find a way to let you know. No college will tell you that you can't apply. Instead, most colleges will find a softer way of breaking the news to you. For instance, they might encourage you to attend another college first and then apply as a transfer student later on. When a college gives you this advice without discussing the likelihood of you being admitted as a transfer student in the future, they are dodging a difficult conversation instead of offering helpful advice. A keeper college will give you specific goals and offer advice for how you can reach them.

Respect Over Popularity

Popularity is largely dependent on superficial qualities, but respect is earned over time through the decisions, behaviors, and accomplishments that reflect character. Schools that are popular are not always well respected, and schools that are well respected aren't always popular. Why? Some schools have incredible respect amongst a small community of professionals, but might not have a lot of name recognition in the general community. Some schools have great name recognition but for totally the wrong reasons, like aggressive advertising. When getting a degree you need to consider what your potential employer will think of the college where you earned your degree.

You might think that it is the degree that matters, not where you earn the degree. In a way you are right, but it depends on your career goals. A degree can get you a foot in the door of a certain field, but where you earn your degree can impact your future earning within that field. Degrees from more prestigious colleges can gain you entrance to more prestigious companies, access to higher levels of advancement, and allow you to command a higher salary. If you think paying people differently depending on where they go to school is elitist and unfair, you are right. It is elitist and it is sometimes blatantly unfair. But the reality is, many employers look at where you went to school as an indicator of what kind of education you received. Schools differ in performance and style the same way cars do. A large truck and a small sedan are designed to do completely different tasks, even if the same manufacturer makes them, and both can deliver goods. The difference being the sedan can deliver pizzas, whereas the truck can haul and deliver a range of goods. The best way to find out what a future employer values is to see whom they have hired in the past. Look at websites of companies you would be interested in working for in the future. See if they have any employee bios or profiles online. If they do, read some over and see what kind of colleges their employees graduated from. You can also check out social networking sites (like LinkedIn) to quickly view professional profiles and see people's academic qualifications.

CHAPTER 2

Cultivating Your Inner Ninja

The road to college success is paved with endless hurdles, especially if you are the first in your family to take the journey. Planning ahead is essential, but so is being flexible when you hit a bump in the road. If you are going to succeed you've got to cultivate your inner college-going ninja. This means being focused, tenacious, and flexible in the face of challenges; approaching every obstacle as a new opportunity for success.

In this chapter you will hear from Lucas, a student who was faced early on in his college search with multiple dead-ends. As you are reading ask yourself how you would have responded if you were in Lucas's place. Why do you think Lucas saw opportunity where others might have only seen disappointment? In the end Lucas chose to take a leap of faith and poured his heart into an unfamiliar opportunity; a decision that probably changed the course of his life forever.

LUCAS

A College Success Story

I was a first generation college student, and so I had no preconceived notion of what a good college was or what a bad college was. I knew Ivy League schools and schools like Northwestern were top tier schools that everyone was striving for, but when it came down to it, my influence on where I wanted to go actually came from YouTube. I used to watch YouTubers.

I would watch them and learn about all their different majors and all their different colleges. I fell in love with the idea of college and all the freedom, experiences, and learning you get to go through.

There was this one person who was into linguistics, and I always found myself watching her videos. I wanted to be cultured; I wanted to learn all the languages; I wanted to visit other countries; and I still want to do that. I was looking into linguistics, and I was looking into the school she went to, which was Florida State University. So when it came around to deciding on colleges, that was one of my first choices for school. I thought it was a beautiful campus. The way she spoke about her classes, the way she talked about the parties, and having friends, I just thought that was something I wanted to be a part of: that community.

The other school I was really interested in was the University of Wisconsin Madison. I had a teacher who went there, and she would just go on about the Badgers, and I thought it sounded amazing. So we visited it, with my advisor. We took the long 3.5 hour drive up there. It was the day before Halloween, and everyone was getting ready for the holiday, and the leaves were changing. I really got a kick out of how the town revolved around the university: to have the townspeople and city hall right down the street. The town was a part of the college, like it was one, big, massive community. Then we walked around the campus, and I knew I would love to be there. I would love to be a part of this. I don't know; I was looking for that textbook experience. I wanted to be that person in the pamphlet; I wanted to be the Latino kid on the diversity poster. That's why those two schools were on the top of my list.

The application process was super different for Florida State and Wisconsin. Florida State eventually required a resume, and I had only worked one job. I didn't have a resume, and it was down to the wire. I was so busy figuring out how to do the resume that I missed the deadline. That was a little bit disappointing. But, I figured it was too far anyway. I always thought I would leave home or whatever, but then I thought about what it actually meant to be that far away. It would be difficult to come home for the holidays; it would be difficult to come home for the summer. I already knew my parents had empty nest syndrome, so I didn't want to put them through that. I wanted to be able to come home. Wisconsin Madison was a great alternative to Florida, but unfortunately I was wait-listed.

I was bummed a little bit, but in our high school class we were talking about the benefits of attending a small school versus a big school. I was reflecting on how I came from a large, public elementary school, and then when I went to a small high school I felt more at home. I felt like I was being educated better in high school than I was in grade school because of the attention I was getting from teachers, because of the smaller classes. I thought, I loved my experience in high school so much I would love to replicate that in college. So when Calbert College appeared on my list of possible schools, I looked at the website. And one thing this school is so proud of is that they are a small campus community. Even though they are close to the city, they are far enough away to be out of that city life. I thought I would get the best of both worlds; I thought I would get that small town atmosphere that I loved about Madison, and I would still get to be away from home, but not too far. So when Madison put me on the wait-list, and Calbert College offered me a generous package, I was like this is a sign. I gotta take it.

After I got accepted, they had an accepted students open house; me, my mom, and my little brother went. We were driving, and we started passing all these mansions, and I was like this is a great area. And then we drove by this sign that said, "middle campus," and there was this big academic building with all these students walking by. I thought this is beautiful. My mom kept saying this must be so expensive here. I didn't care. We were walking up to the campus and we were surrounded by the forest. And then we walked ten minutes east and there was this private beach just for students, for free. It was one of the most beautiful beaches I had ever seen.

I got to sit in on a class, and I actually felt like I knew what they were talking about. I felt like my high school had prepared me for that experience. And they allowed me to participate, so I raised my hand and offered my two-cents every once in a while. I felt a part of the class. And it was such a small class, like 15 students. They were talking about a book that I had never read before, but I was able to add to the conversation.

By and large, the faculty is the most supportive and encouraging group of people I have known in my entire life. I have never met a staff member that didn't want you to succeed. Not to say that I have never had positive supports, but there is so much here it is overwhelming. And it's not just professors and faculty, but the staff and leadership we have too. We have someone that connects you to resources in Chicago. We have a math resource center and a writing center where students and faculty come help other students learn math and science better. There are language tables where language proficiency professors will have lunch with the students and talk in Spanish or French. And, it has nothing to do with the class; it just has to do with building relationships with the students.

I think one of the greatest professors I've had was a history professor I had as a freshmen. He noticed my attentiveness and how much I appreciated the class, and he would invite me to his office sometimes. He asked me if I had ever considered being a history major and offered to be my advisor. It is not uncommon for a professor to invite students to their home. Some professors actually live on campus, or not far from the campus, and they will invite students to dinner in their home, or organize a trip to Chicago.

I didn't know what I wanted to do when I went into college. I knew what I liked to do; I knew I liked history and politics, and I knew I wanted to travel and experience different cultures. So I thought international relations sounded great. I wanted to work at the UN and be involved in politics. When I started learning about what actually happens in the field, I began to question whether I would be happy doing that, or if it would *just be a job. I wanted to do something that would make me happy. At liberal arts schools, at least here, you have the time and resources to explore other options and see where you fit in in the world, and what you want to do.*

I became an RA to save money on housing on campus. I didn't think that becoming an RA would make me want to get involved in student affairs, but it did. At the same time that I was an RA I was on the college programming board, where I was vice president of programming. I also had a good relationship with the Intercultural Relationships office, because the director was my advisor. After seeing all the work that the different offices did, I realized I wanted to get involved in student affairs. I wanted to work in higher education, which is completely different from what I wanted to do before. Now I am looking into what it takes to work in higher education, or in secondary education—possibly as a vice-principal.

I definitely thought about graduate school, where I would go, and what experience I wanted to have. A lot of students here are talking about going to Northwestern, or Yale, or other big schools. I think it would be a completely different experience. I don't want to say that I have been coddled here, but it would be a new environment. Of course, that was the environment that I sought out before, but I have become enamored with the small school environment. I've loved being in a small liberal arts school so much, I don't know how I would do going to a large school. I'm not sure I want to be in a lecture hall with 300 students. One of the things I love about here is that with such small classes, even if the professor doesn't speak directly to me I feel comfortable enough turning to my neighbor and asking, "Do you mind helping me out?" Being in a large school would be out of my comfort zone, but then again, for the last three years all I've done is be out of my comfort zone.

I think it is so much easier to change your position if you are a blank canvas. If you think of the analogy of a canvas, it is much easier to start painting on a blank canvas than it is to erase what you already started painting and start something new. So I would encourage students to keep their minds open and always stay receptive to taking a new opportunity that you didn't think you would have taken, because that one might be the opportunity that changes your life for the better. You might enter a new experience that you never would have thought of, and the next thing you know you want to do it for the rest of your life, like I have.*

It's What's On the Inside that Counts

Lucas is a great example of a college success story. He didn't just earn a degree; he developed into a fuller and more actualized version of himself. The academic rigor of the college seemed to be a perfect match—not too difficult, but not too easy either. The faculty cared about his success in life (not just in their classes), and they invested in him to cultivate that success. He had access to a plethora of academic services and social activities to support his success in college. Lucas wasn't just a student at a college; he was a member of a college family.

In an ideal world, I would want every student to experience what Lucas was able to experience: a college that developed him academically, intellectually, and personally. But, the reality is, not every student can have what Lucas had. As much as it pains me to say, there are limited spaces available at high quality institutions like the one Lucas attended. It is one of my career goals to change the landscape of higher education so all students have access to top-notch colleges and universities. Until that happens, the best I can do is provide you with the tools necessary to ensure that you have the best possible options on the table when it comes time to finally make a decision.

Lucas's story is a story about learning—not just learning in college, but learning about college. One of the first things Lucas shares with us is that he is a first generation college student. He isn't just providing us with insight into his family history; he is acknowledging that his story might sound a little funny to those who come from a family where going to college is common place. In Lucas's family, going to college was not common. He didn't grow up hearing stories about college. He didn't get to hear about the pranks his uncle used to play on his buddies in the dorm, or how his mom had to deal with a sexist professor, or how his sister had to sit in on double classes for two weeks trying to get "added" to a pre-requisite class. He didn't hear those stories because those things never happened. As a result, Lucas had little to no information on where to begin the college search process. So, he began his search online.

YouTube made the world of college real for Lucas. Listening to other students' experiences allowed him to imagine himself at college—imagine the struggles, the fun, the academic experiences, etc. In turn, Lucas' story now allows you to imagine what it would be like to go to a little college by the beach, where professors invite you to their homes for dinner, students practice their French at lunch, and where your opinions actually matter in the classroom.

As much as Lucas's story is about the importance of college exposure, it is also about keeping an open mind. You may find attending a small liberal arts school like Lucas's really appealing. Or, you might decide that a different type of school is a better fit for you. No matter what your final decision, keep your options open. Be curious. Take the time to listen to other people's stories. Take the time to imagine yourself in their shoes. Get to know yourself and your needs. Get to know different colleges, their limitations, and what they have to offer. Don't allow yourself to be distracted by superficial characteristics (ahem...Florida beach). Instead, look at the substance of a college. Ask yourself: what would I need to be happy at this school? What would I need to be successful here?

BREAK IT DOWN!
Lucas

- *Why do you think Lucas was so set on Florida State and Wisconsin, Madison?*
- *What happened that made Lucas consider other options?*
- *What do you think would have happened to Lucas if he had only applied to his top two choices?*
- *How does Lucas's story make you feel (hopeful, nervous, happy, uncomfortable, angry, excited)? Why?*

Chapter 3

Your College Application Strategy

With thousands of colleges and universities in the U.S., how do you reduce your college choices down to a list of twenty or so you should actually consider? Narrowing your college search takes some honest self-reflection about who you are and what is really important to you. Having too many "must haves" can be as much of a misstep as not having any. Unreasonable expectations and unnecessary restrictions will just leave you with a big pile of "nos" without any "yeses." Alternatively, if you don't limit your search at all you are going to end up wading through some real duds before you get to some legitimate possibilities. So what criteria should you be using to narrow your college search?

This is where the concept of college match can be really helpful. Now, there is an entire field of research around college match that asks some very theoretical questions about students, colleges, and their odds of success together. However, for our purposes, it helps to think about college match as a tool to maximize your chances of being admitted to the best schools you can get into. When I say "best schools" I don't mean the schools that you will be most satisfied with. When I say "best schools" I am really talking about a combination of effectiveness (graduation rate), affordability, and prestige mixed into one. Based on your test scores and GPA, you have a range of schools that you are likely to get into; these are your match schools.

Finding match schools requires focusing your attention on colleges that traditionally admit students who have similar grades and test scores as you. This does not mean that you *will* get admitted; it just means that your grades and test scores *won't keep you* from getting admitted. Schools that are less selective traditionally admit students with lower GPAs and lower test scores, and also tend to have less prestige and lower graduation rates. Schools that are more selective tend to admit students with higher GPAs and higher test scores, and tend to have greater prestige and higher graduation rates. The more selective the school, the pickier they can be about who they admit.

You might think you should just apply to the most selective schools possible; that way if you get in you will be going to a really high quality school. As great as this strategy sounds, it's not a really good way to approach applying to college. Why? Because the chance of being admitted to a highly selective school is not good. You need to mix it up! You need to be thoughtful and apply to a number of strategically chosen colleges. So, how do you know which colleges to apply to? If you apply to schools that you are interested in without considering if they are interested in you, your chances of success are pretty slim. What you want to do is decide which colleges to apply to based on how likely you are to be admitted, how likely it is to be affordable, and how likely you are to graduate from that college.

Doing your research on colleges is important. But even with all the information in the world, there are things you just can't account for, like whether or not you will actually be admitted and how much in scholarships the school will offer you. Because there are so many unknowns in the college admissions process, you want to include a range of schools that vary in selectivity (admissions rate/graduation rate), location (in-state, out-of state), and type (public, liberal arts, etc.). This ensures that you have a good range of options when it comes time to finally decide. In the next section, you will look up your specific qualifications to find your **Match Strategy**. Your Match Strategy is going to maximize your probability of being admitted to a range of schools that vary in prestige and cost.

Before we get to your match strategy, let's take a moment and build a common language around college. In the next few pages you will find a glossary of terms. One of the major concepts covered is a term I call "college axis." A college's axis is really just a way to categorize the average test-scores and GPA of the students who attend that college. By categorizing colleges into axes, we can focus your attention on a smaller pool of colleges that match your academic profile in high school. Within any particular axis category there are a ridiculous number of colleges—so many in fact you couldn't even apply to all of them if you wanted to. Focusing on a particular axis isn't about limiting your options; it is about maximizing your efforts. Who wants to spend time applying to ten or twenty colleges that you have no prayer of getting admitted to? Not me, and I am guessing not you either!

Don't worry about memorizing the axis categories. Just read them over once to get the concept. In a nutshell, schools that admit students with the highest average test-scores and highest GPAs will be near Axis 1. Schools that admit students with lower average test-scores and lower GPAs will be closer to Axis 5. Axis 6 and Axis 7 programs do not have GPA or ACT/SAT requirements; these are open-access opportunities. You will also find a list of types of colleges. This is a small list, so take the time to read it carefully.

Chapter 4

Strategy Glossary

College Axis

- **Axis 1 Plus**: These are schools where the middle 50 percent of admitted students had GPAs of 3.7 or above, ACTs of 28 or above, and SATs of 1370 or above (1930 in the old 2400 point system). Don't worry if your test scores are a little lower than the school's average. Examples: *Northwestern University (private), Williams College (liberal arts), Johns Hopkins University (private), Pomona College (liberal arts), University of Virginia (public), University of Pennsylvania (private).*

- **Axis 1**: These are schools where the middle 50 percent of admitted students had GPAs of 3.6 or above, ACTs of 26 or above, and SATs of 1270 or above (1780 in the old 2400 point system). Don't worry if your test scores are a little lower than the school's average. Examples: *Boston University (private), University of Michigan (public), Denison University (liberal arts), Lewis and Clark College (liberal arts), DePauw University (liberal arts).*

- **Axis 2**: These are schools where the middle 50 percent of admitted students had GPAs above 3.3, ACTs of 24 or above, and SATs of 1200 above (1670 in the old 2400 point system). Don't worry if your test scores are a little lower than the school's average. Examples: *University of Colorado, Boulder (public), Beloit College (liberal arts), Xavier University (private), University of Dayton (private), University of Delaware (public).*

- **Axis 3**: These are schools where the middle 50 percent of admitted students had GPAs of 3.0 or above, ACTs of 21 or above, and SATs of 1090 or above (1490 in the old 2400 point system). Don't worry if your test scores are a little lower than the school's average. Examples: *University of Memphis (public), Boise State University (public), Eastern Illinois University (public), Carthage College (liberal arts), Spelman College (HBCU), Howard University (HBCU), Viterbo University (private).*

- **Axis 4**: These are schools where the middle 50 percent of admitted students had GPAs of 2.5 or above, ACTs of 18 or above; and SATs of 1000 or above (1360 in the old 2400 point system). Don't worry if your test scores are a little lower than the schools average.

- **Axis 5**: These are schools where the middle 50 percent of admitted students had GPAs of 2.0 or above; ACT of 16 or above, and SATs of 950 or above (1290 in the old 2400 point system). Don't worry if your test scores are a little lower than the school's average.

- **Axis 6**: Open access, two-year colleges/community colleges. These colleges are usually public colleges and offer the chance to pursue your higher education at a very low cost. These colleges offer certificate programs, Associates of Arts degrees, and transfer opportunities.

- **Axis 7**: Workforce development. These are programs that focus on building a particular set of skills to help you get a job.

Types of Colleges

- **In-State College:** Colleges located in your state. Many states offer state grants to use towards in-state schools, sometimes making them more affordable.

- **Liberal Arts College:** Liberal arts colleges are colleges that focus on a holistic and well-rounded undergraduate education. These schools tend to value diversity and often provide good financial aid for low-income students.

- **Private College:** Private colleges are any college that is not a public institution (one funded by the state). You can find out if a school is private by looking them up on https://collegescorecard.ed.gov. Private schools are great, but avoid for-profit-schools.

- **Public Colleges:** Colleges that receive state funding. These schools are public institutions and offer residents of that state reduced tuition.

- **GPA Indexed College:** Colleges that allow students to make up a weaker test score with a stronger GPA, and a weaker GPA with a stronger test score.

- **Test-Optional Colleges:** Colleges that allow you to apply without test-scores. These schools will weigh your GPA heavily and will often ask for additional essays or letters of recommendation in place of test scores.

- **Historically Black Colleges and Universities (HBCU):** HBCUs are colleges that have a historical mission of educating African American students. There are more than 100 HBCUs in the United States with a wide range of admissions criteria. For a complete list of HBCUs visit sites.ed.gov/whhbcu.

Some prominent HBCU attendees include:
- Toni Morrison (Nobel Prize winning author), Howard University
- Reverend Jesse Jackson (civil rights leader, activist), North Carolina A&T
- Oprah Winfrey (entertainment mogul), Tennessee State University
- Common (musician, actor, producer), Florida A&M
- Spike Lee (producer, director), Morehouse College
- Eryka Badu (musician), Grambling State University
- Samuel L. Jackson (actor), Morehouse College
- Jerry Rice (NFL athlete), Mississippi Valley State University
- Pam Oliver (sports commentator), Florida A&M University
- Wanda Sykes (comedian, actor), Hampton University
- Keshia Knight-Pulliam (actor), Spelman College

Identifying Your Application Strategy

Identifying your application strategy is actually very simple. You will only need two criteria to determine your application strategy: your unweighted GPA and your ACT or SAT composite score. The application strategy here is just a starting point. You should feel free to add as many colleges as you would like that fall outside of the application strategy. I do suggest, though, that you start with schools that fit your application strategy and then complete applications for additional schools afterwards. It is also important to remember that there are thousands of colleges in the US, and the lists of schools provided in this chapter are just examples that fit the provided criteria. **Do not limit yourself only to schools on the lists provided.** Feel free to widen your search as much as you like. Now, let's get started.

Easy as 1,2,3

Fill in the blanks below with your GPA and standardized test scores. For GPA, lookup your most recent unweighted, cumulative GPA (this is most likely the GPA you had at the end of Junior year). Make sure it is unweighted, and cumulative. You can look at your most recent report card, or ask your school counselor for the information. Next, look up your highest ACT or SAT composite score.

❶ My cumulative GPA _____

❷ My highest composite score _____

❸ To locate your application strategy, start by finding the section that corresponds to your cumulative, unweighted GPA. Then look up the page that corresponds to your test score.

GPA 3.5+

ACT Under 16 / SAT 900 and under**

When filling out your list, DO NOT limit yourself to the colleges listed in this book! Instead, use these colleges as examples to help guide your search.

- 2 Test-Optional colleges (in-state if possible)

  _____
  _____
  _____
  _____

- 2 GPA-Indexed colleges (in-state if possible)

  _____
  _____
  _____
  _____

- 2 Axis 4, Public colleges (in-state)

  _____
  _____
  _____
  _____

* Ask your counselor for a fee waiver to retake your SAT/ACT. Sign up for the SAT/ACT. Set a goal to increase your score by 2+ points. Use FREE websites like www.khanacademy.org to help you study.

GPA 3.5+

ACT 16-17 / SAT 910-990**

When filling out your list, DO NOT limit yourself to the colleges listed in this book! Instead, use these colleges as examples to help guide your search.

- 2 Test-Optional colleges (in-state if possible)

  _____
  _____
  _____
  _____

- 2 GPA-Indexed colleges (in-state if possible)

  _____
  _____
  _____
  _____

- 2 Axis 4, Private colleges

  _____
  _____
  _____
  _____

- 2 Axis 4, Public colleges (in-state)

  _____
  _____
  _____
  _____

* Ask your counselor for a fee waiver to retake your SAT/ACT. Sign up for the SAT/ACT. Set a goal to increase your score by 2+ points. Use FREE websites like www.khanacademy.org to help you study.

GPA 3.5+

ACT 18-21 / SAT 1000-1130

When filling out your list, DO NOT limit yourself to the colleges listed in this book! Instead, use these colleges as examples to help guide your search.

- 1 Axis 2, Liberal arts college

  _____
  _____
  _____

- 2 Axis 3, Private colleges

  _____
  _____
  _____

- 1 Axis 3, Public college (in-state)

  _____
  _____
  _____

- 1 Axis 4, Public college (in-state)

  _____
  _____
  _____

- 2 Test-Optional colleges (in-state if possible)

  _____
  _____
  _____

GPA 3.5+

ACT 22-24 / SAT 1140-1230

When filling out your list, DO NOT limit yourself to the colleges listed in this book! Instead, use these colleges as examples to help guide your search.

- Apply to Posse, Gates Millennium or Quest Bridge

_____
_____
_____

- 2 Axis 1, Liberal arts colleges

_____
_____
_____

- 1 Axis 2, Public college (in-state)

_____
_____
_____

- 1 Axis 2, Private or liberal arts college (in-state)

_____
_____
_____

- 1 Axis 3, Private college

_____
_____
_____

- 1 Axis 3, Public college (in-state)

_____
_____
_____

GPA 3.5+

ACT 25+ / SAT 1240+

When filling out your list, DO NOT limit yourself to the colleges listed in this book! Instead, use these colleges as examples to help guide your search.

- Apply to Posse, Gates Millennium or Quest Bridge
  _____
  _____

- 1 Axis 1 PLUS, Research college
  _____
  _____

- 1 Axis 1 PLUS, Liberal arts college
  _____
  _____

- 2 Axis 1, Liberal arts colleges
  _____
  _____

- 1 Axis 2, Private college (in-state)
  _____
  _____

- 1 Axis 2, Public college (in-state)
  _____
  _____

- 1 Axis 3, Public college (in-state)
  _____
  _____

GPA 3.0-3.49

ACT Under 16 / SAT 900 and under**

When filling out your list, DO NOT limit yourself to the colleges listed in this book! Instead, use these colleges as examples to help guide your search.

- 2 Test-Optional colleges (in-state if possible)

  _____
  _____
  _____
  _____

- 2 Axis 5, Private colleges (in-state)

  _____
  _____
  _____
  _____

- 2 Axis 5, Public colleges (in-state)

  _____
  _____
  _____
  _____

* Ask your counselor for a fee waiver to retake your SAT/ACT. Sign up for the SAT/ACT. Set a goal to increase your score by 2+ points. Use FREE websites like www.khanacademy.org to help you study.

GPA 3.0-3.49

ACT 16-17 / SAT 910-990**

When filling out your list, DO NOT limit yourself to the colleges listed in this book! Instead, use these colleges as examples to help guide your search.

- 2 Test-Optional colleges (in-state if possible)

  _____
  _____
  _____

- 1 Axis 4, Private college (in-state)

  _____
  _____
  _____

- 1 Axis 5, Private college (in-state)

  _____
  _____
  _____

- 1 Axis 5, Public college (in-state)

  _____
  _____
  _____

* Ask your counselor for a fee waiver to retake your SAT/ACT. Sign up for the SAT/ACT. Set a goal to increase your score by 2+ points. Use FREE websites like www.khanacademy.org to help you study.

GPA 3.0-3.49

ACT 18-21 / SAT 1000-1130

When filling out your list, DO NOT limit yourself to the colleges listed in this book! Instead, use these colleges as examples to help guide your search.

- 1 Axis 2, Public college (in-state)

  _____
  _____
  _____

- 1 Axis 3, Public college (in-state)

  _____
  _____
  _____

- 1 Axis 3, Private college (in-state)

  _____
  _____
  _____

- 1 Axis 4, Public college (in-state)

  _____
  _____
  _____

- 1 Axis 4, Private college (in-state)

  _____
  _____
  _____

GPA 3.0-3.49

ACT 22-24 / SAT 1140-1230

When filling out your list, DO NOT limit yourself to the colleges listed in this book! Instead, use these colleges as examples to help guide your search.

- Apply to Posse, Gates Millennium or Quest Bridge
  _____
  _____

- 1 Axis 2, Liberal arts college
  _____
  _____

- 1 Axis 2, Public college (in-state)
  _____
  _____

- 1 Axis 2, Private college (in-state)
  _____
  _____

- 1 Axis 3, Private college
  _____
  _____

- 1 Axis 3, Private college (in-state)
  _____
  _____

- 1 Axis 3, Public college (in-state)
  _____
  _____

GPA 3.0-3.49

ACT 25+ / SAT 1240+

When filling out your list, DO NOT limit yourself to the colleges listed in this book! Instead, use these colleges as examples to help guide your search.

- Apply to Posse, Gates Millennium or Quest Bridge
  _____
  _____

- 2 Axis 2, Liberal arts colleges
  _____
  _____

- 1 Axis 2, Public college (in-state)
  _____
  _____

- 1 Axis 2, Private college (in-state)
  _____
  _____

- 1 Axis 3, Private college
  _____
  _____

- 1 Axis 3, Public college (in-state)
  _____
  _____

- 1 Axis 3, Private college (in-state)
  _____
  _____

GPA 2.5-2.99

ACT Under 16 / SAT 900 and under**

When filling out your list, DO NOT limit yourself to the colleges listed in this book! Instead, use these colleges as examples to help guide your search.

- 2 Axis 5, Public colleges (in-state)

  _____
  _____
  _____
  _____

- 2 Axis 6, Colleges or tech programs

  _____
  _____
  _____
  _____

* Ask your counselor for a fee waiver to retake your SAT/ACT. Sign up for the SAT/ACT. Set a goal to increase your score by 2+ points. Use FREE websites like www.khanacademy.org to help you study.

GPA 2.5-2.99

ACT 16-17* / SAT 910-990*

When filling out your list, DO NOT limit yourself to the colleges listed in this book! Instead, use these colleges as examples to help guide your search.

- 1 Axis 3, Public college (in-state)

  _____
  _____
  _____
  _____

- 2 Axis 4, Public colleges (in-state)

  _____
  _____
  _____
  _____

- 1 Axis 5, Public college (in-state)

  _____
  _____
  _____
  _____

- 1 Axis 6, College

  _____
  _____
  _____
  _____

* Ask your counselor for a fee waiver to retake your SAT/ACT. Sign up for the SAT/ACT. Set a goal to increase your score by 2+ points. Use FREE websites like www.khanacademy.org to help you study.

GPA 2.5-2.99

ACT 18-21 / SAT 1000-1130

When filling out your list, DO NOT limit yourself to the colleges listed in this book! Instead, use these colleges as examples to help guide your search.

- 2 Axis 3, Public colleges (in-state)

  _____
  _____
  _____

- 1 Axis 3, Private college

  _____
  _____
  _____

- 1 Axis 4, Private college (in-state)

  _____
  _____
  _____

- 2 Axis 4, Public colleges (in-state)

  _____
  _____
  _____

- 1 Axis 5, Public college (in-state)

  _____
  _____
  _____

GPA 2.5-2.99

ACT 22-24 / SAT 1140-1230

When filling out your list, DO NOT limit yourself to the colleges listed in this book! Instead, use these colleges as examples to help guide your search.

- 1 Axis 3, Private college

  _____
  _____
  _____

- 2 Axis 3, Public colleges (in-state)

  _____
  _____
  _____

- 1 Axis 4, Private college (in-state)

  _____
  _____
  _____

- 2 Axis 4, Public colleges (in-state)

  _____
  _____
  _____

GPA 2.5-2.99

ACT 25+ / SAT 1240+

When filling out your list, DO NOT limit yourself to the colleges listed in this book! Instead, use these colleges as examples to help guide your search.

- 1 Axis 2, Liberal arts college

  _____
  _____
  _____

- 2 Axis 3, Private colleges

  _____
  _____
  _____

- 2 Axis 3, Public colleges (in-state)

  _____
  _____
  _____

- 1 Axis 3, Private college (in-state)

  _____
  _____
  _____

- 1 Axis 4, Public college (in-state)

  _____
  _____
  _____

GPA 2.0-2.49

ACT Under 16 / SAT 900 and under**

When filling out your list, DO NOT limit yourself to the colleges listed in this book! Instead, use these colleges as examples to help guide your search.

- 2 Axis 6, Colleges or tech programs

  _____
  _____
  _____
  _____

- 2 Axis 7, Programs

  _____
  _____
  _____
  _____

* Ask your counselor for a fee waiver to retake your SAT/ACT. Sign up for the SAT/ACT. Set a goal to increase your score by 2+ points. Use FREE websites like www.khanacademy.org to help you study.

GPA 2.0-2.49

ACT 16-17 / SAT 910-990**

When filling out your list, DO NOT limit yourself to the colleges listed in this book! Instead, use these colleges as examples to help guide your search.

- 1 Axis 5, Public college (in-state)

  _____
  _____
  _____
  _____

- 2 Axis 6, Colleges

  _____
  _____
  _____
  _____

- 1 Axis 7, Program

  _____
  _____
  _____
  _____

* Ask your counselor for a fee waiver to retake your SAT/ACT. Sign up for the SAT/ACT. Set a goal to increase your score by 2+ points. Use FREE websites like www.khanacademy.org to help you study.

GPA 2.0-2.49

ACT 18-21 / SAT 1000-1130

When filling out your list, DO NOT limit yourself to the colleges listed in this book! Instead, use these colleges as examples to help guide your search.

- 2 Axis 4, Public colleges (in-state)

  _____
  _____
  _____
  _____

- 1 Axis 5, Public college (in-state)

  _____
  _____
  _____

- 1 GPA-Indexed college (in-state, if possible)

  _____
  _____
  _____
  _____

- 1 Axis 6, College

  _____
  _____
  _____
  _____

GPA 2.0-2.49

ACT 22-24 / SAT 1140-1230

When filling out your list, DO NOT limit yourself to the colleges listed in this book! Instead, use these colleges as examples to help guide your search.

- 3 GPA-Indexed colleges (in-state, if possible)

  _____
  _____
  _____
  _____

- 2 Axis 4, Public colleges (in-state)

  _____
  _____
  _____
  _____

- 1 Axis 5, Public college (in-state)

  _____
  _____
  _____
  _____

- 1 Axis 6, College

  _____
  _____
  _____
  _____

GPA 2.0-2.49

ACT 25+ / SAT 1240+

When filling out your list, DO NOT limit yourself to the colleges listed in this book! Instead, use these colleges as examples to help guide your search.

- 3 GPA-Indexed colleges (in-state, if possible)

_____
_____
_____
_____

- 2 Axis 4, Public colleges (in-state)

_____
_____
_____
_____

- 1 Axis 5, Public college (in-state)

_____
_____
_____
_____

GPA Under 2.0

ACT Under 18 / SAT Under 1000

When filling out your list, DO NOT limit yourself to the colleges listed in this book! Instead, use these colleges as examples to help guide your search.

- 3 Axis 6, Technical training programs (non-profit)

  _____
  _____
  _____
  _____

- 2 Axis 7 Programs

  _____
  _____
  _____
  _____

GPA Under 2.0

ACT 18-21 / SAT 1000-1130

When filling out your list, DO NOT limit yourself to the colleges listed in this book! Instead, use these colleges as examples to help guide your search.

- 1 GPA-Indexed college (in-state, if possible)

  _____
  _____
  _____
  _____

- 2 Axis 6, Technical training program (non-profit)

  _____
  _____
  _____
  _____

- 1 Axis 7 Program

  _____
  _____
  _____
  _____

GPA Under 2.0

ACT 22-24 / SAT 1140-1230

When filling out your list, DO NOT limit yourself to the colleges listed in this book! Instead, use these colleges as examples to help guide your search.

- 2 GPA-Indexed college (in-state, if possible)

　

- 2 Axis 5, Colleges (in-state)

　

- 2 Axis 6, Colleges

GPA Under 2.0

ACT 25+ / SAT 1240+

When filling out your list, DO NOT limit yourself to the colleges listed in this book! Instead, use these colleges as examples to help guide your search.

- 2 GPA-Indexed colleges (in-state, if possible)

_____
_____
_____
_____

- 1 Axis 4, Public college (in-state)

_____
_____
_____
_____

- 2 Axis 5, Colleges (in-state)

_____
_____
_____
_____

- 1 Axis 6, College

_____
_____
_____
_____

CHAPTER 5

Using Your College Application Strategy

Congratulations! Do you realize what you have just done? You've completed a HUGE and important step in your college search! One of the most difficult and frustrating parts of the application process is figuring out where you should apply. You may not have the school names filled in yet, but you have done a lot of work just by identifying a strategy. You can now speak confidently to anyone and everyone about your college application process.

> **EXAMPLE**
>
> "I am not sure where I want to go to college yet, but I know I want to apply to a few liberal arts schools and a couple in-state public schools."
>
> Don't you sound like you are on your game? And guess what? YOU ARE! Now it's time to figure out how to put your college application strategy to use.

Once you have found your application strategy, use it as a guide to identify possible colleges. Don't expect that you will be able to fill in your list in a single day, or even a week. Give yourself time. Identifying your state schools will probably be the easiest, so start there. After that it is really up to you. Some of the categories (liberal arts schools, GPA-indexed colleges, and test-optional colleges) will have reference lists in

Chapter 7. Other categories, like in-state public, in-state private schools, Axis 6 schools, and Axis 7 programs won't have lists; there are just too many schools to include. Instead, the best way to approach these is to use the Department of Education's College Scorecard website (https://collegescorecard.ed.gov) as outlined in Chapter 6.

Take a Breather

If you are ready to tackle your college application list, you can dive right in to Chapters 6 and 7. Otherwise, feel free to skip ahead to Chapter 8. In Chapters 8 and 9 we are going to hear about other students' experiences in college. Like Elena and Lucas, every college student has a story to share. You will too, one day. Hopefully, the experiences of the students in Chapters 8 and 9 will help you think about exactly what kind of college you want to attend.

Chapter 6

Finding Colleges for Your Strategy

It's a good idea to set aside about a month to select the specific colleges for your college application list. Your application strategy provides the parameters, but you still need to choose the specific colleges you want to apply to. This chapter provides some basic lists of nationally ranked colleges to get you started. Most colleges are listed by Axis and type (see below). As mentioned previously, don't limit yourself to what's in this book. As you are searching college options online, you may stumble across a great find that isn't in this book. That's wonderful! Just make sure to look up the average test scores and GPA of admitted students, and make sure it is a not-for-profit school.

In-State, Public Colleges (Axis 1 through Axis 5)

Go to the U.S. Department of Education College Scorecard website at https://collegescorecard.ed.gov.

❶ Under PROGRAMS AND DEGREES select FOUR YEAR.

❷ Under LOCATION select your state (leave the rest of the options blank).

❸ Under ADVANCED SEARCH select PUBLIC for type of school. Click FIND SCHOOLS.

❹ SORT your results by GRADUATION RATE.

❺ Select a school and then click VIEW MORE DETAILS. You will see important information about the school including location, graduation rate, average income after graduation, and admissions information.

❻ Scroll down and click "SAT/ACT scores." You will see a green bar between two numbers. This is the average SAT/ACT range. If the SAT/ACT range falls within one of the axes on your strategy, then this school might be a possible match for you. Check out the graduation rate (higher is better) and the average debt (less is better). Spend as much time as you need until you have found the schools that have the best graduation rates for your strategy.

In-State, Private Colleges (Axis 1 through Axis 5)

Go to the U.S. Department of Education College Scorecard website at https://collegescorecard.ed.gov.

❶ Under PROGRAMS AND DEGREES select FOUR YEAR.

❷ Under LOCATION select your state (leave the rest of the options blank).

❸ Under ADVANCED SEARCH select PRIVATE, **NON-PROFIT** for type of school. Click FIND SCHOOLS.

❹ SORT your results by GRADUATION RATE.

❺ Select a school and then click VIEW MORE DETAILS. You will see important information about the school including location, graduation rate, average income after graduation, and admissions information.

6 Scroll down and click "SAT/ACT scores." You will see a green bar between two numbers. This is the average SAT/ACT range. If the SAT/ACT range falls within one of the axes on your strategy, then this school might be a possible match for you. Check out the graduation rate (higher is better) and the average debt (less is better). Spend as much time as you need until you have found the schools that have the best graduation rates for your strategy.

Community Colleges (Axis 6)

Go to the U.S. Department of Education College Scorecard website at https://collegescorecard.ed.gov.

1 Under PROGRAMS AND DEGREES select TWO YEAR.

2 Under LOCATION select your state (leave the rest of the options blank).

3 Under ADVANCED SEARCH select PUBLIC for type of school. Click FIND SCHOOLS.

4 SORT your results by GRADUATION RATE.

5 Select a school and then click VIEW MORE DETAILS. You will see important information about the school including location, graduation rate, average income after graduation, and admissions information.

6 Check out the graduation rate (higher is better) and the average debt (less is better). Spend as much time as you need until you have found the schools that have the best graduation rates for your strategy.

Most students will not relocate to attend a community college. If you are considering relocating, make sure you have a solid plan for where you will live and how you will pay for rent, food, etc. in your new area.

Workforce Development Programs (Axis 7)

Go to the U.S. Department of Labor's Career One Stop website at http://www.careeronestop.org.

❶ Click "find training."

❷ Enter in the type of technical career you are looking for and the location (city, state you live in).

❸ Scroll down on the left and select the length of training program you would like. I suggest either "less than one year" or "at least one but less than two."

Look through the program names and locations. The link will take you to the program/school's website to get more information. Sometimes it is just easier to call the school directly and ask how you apply for the particular program you are interested in.

CHAPTER 7

College Lists

In the next few pages you will find lists that correspond to the different sections of your college application strategy. They include:

- Axis 1 PLUS Research Universities (page 73)
- Axis 1 PLUS Liberal Arts Colleges (page 74)
- Axis 1 Research Universities (page 75)
- Axis 1 Liberal Arts Colleges (page 76)
- Axis 2 Research Universities (page 77)
- Axis 2 Liberal Arts Colleges (page 79)
- Axis 3 Private Liberal Arts Schools (page 81)
- Test Optional Colleges (page 82)
- GPA Indexed Colleges (page 83-page 85)

Axis 1 PLUS Research Universities

MA	Brandeis University
RI	Brown University
CA	California Institute of Technology
PA	Carnegie Mellon University
VA	College of William and Mary
NY	Columbia University in the City of New York
NY	Cornell University
NH	Dartmouth College
NC	Duke University
GA	Emory University
DC	Georgetown University
MA	Harvard University
MD	Johns Hopkins University
PA	Lehigh University
MA	Massachusetts Institute of Technology
NY	New York University
IL	Northwestern University
NJ	Princeton University
TX	Rice University
CA	Stanford University
MA	Tufts University
LA	Tulane University of Louisiana
CA	University of California-Berkeley
IL	University of Chicago
IN	University of Notre Dame
PA	University of Pennsylvania
CA	University of Southern California
TN	Vanderbilt University
MO	Washington University in St Louis
CT	Yale University

Axis 1 PLUS Liberal Arts Colleges

ME	Amherst College
NY	Bard College
NY	Barnard College
ME	Bates College
ME	Bowdoin College
PA	Bucknell University
MN	Carleton College
CA	Claremont McKenna College
ME	Colby College
NY	Colgate University
CO	Colorado College
NC	Davidson College
PA	Gettysburg College
IO	Grinnell College
NY	Hamilton College
CA	Harvey Mudd College
PA	Haverford College
OH	Kenyon College
MN	Macalester College
VT	Middlebury College
OH	Oberlin College
OR	Reed College
CA	Scripps College
PA	Swarthmore College
NY	Vassar College
VA	Washington and Lee University
MA	Wellesley College
CT	Wesleyan University
MA	Williams College

Axis 1 Research Universities

DC	American University
TX	Baylor University
TN	Belmont University (TN)
MA	Boston University
OH	Case Western Reserve University
MA	Clark University
NC	Elon University
NY	Fordham University
DC	George Washington University
IL	Illinois Institute of Technology
IN	Indiana University-Bloomington
CA	Pepperdine University
IN	Rutgers University-New Brunswick
CA	Santa Clara University
NY	Syracuse University
TX	Trinity University
CO	University of Colorado Boulder
IL	University of Illinois at Urbana-Champaign
FL	University of Miami
MI	University of Michigan-Ann Arbor
MN	University of Minnesota-Twin Cities
PA	University of Pittsburgh-Pittsburgh Campus
CA	University of San Diego
WA	University of Washington-Seattle Campus
WI	University of Wisconsin-Madison
VA	Virginia Polytechnic Institute and State University
NC	Wake Forest University
MA	Worcester Polytechnic Institute

Axis 1 Liberal Arts Colleges

GA	Agnes Scott College (women's)
PA	Bryn Mawr College (women's)
MA	College of the Holy Cross
OH	College of Wooster
CT	Connecticut College
OH	Denison University
IN	DePauw University
PA	Dickinson College
MA	Emerson College
PA	Franklin and Marshall College
SC	Furman University
IL	Illinois Wesleyan University
PA	Lafayette College
OR	Lewis & Clark College
MA	Mount Holyoke College
CA	Occidental College
CA	Pitzer College
TN	Rhodes College
NY	Sarah Lawrence College
TN	Sewanee-The University of the South
NY	Skidmore College
MA	Smith College
WI	St. Lawrence University
MD	St. Mary's College of Maryland
MN	St. Olaf College
CT	Trinity College
WA	University of Puget Sound
PA	Ursinus College

Axis 2 Research Universities

AL	Auburn University
CA	Azusa Pacific University
CA	Biola University
IN	Butler University
NY	Clarkson University
CO	Colorado State -Fort Collins (public)
IL	DePaul University
PA	Drexel University
NY	Hofstra University
DC	Howard University (HBCU)
IO	Iowa State University
KS	Kansas State University
IL	Loyola University Chicago
WI	Marquette University
OH	Miami University-Oxford (public)
MI	Michigan State University (public)
MO	Missouri State -Springfield (public)
IN	Purdue University (public)
AL	Samford University
WA	Seattle University
NJ	Seton Hall University
FL	Stetson University
PA	Temple University (public)
TX	Texas Christian University
AZ	University of Arizona (public)
CA	Univ of California-Riverside (public)
OH	University of Dayton
CO	University of Denver
ME	University of Maine (public)
MN	University of Minnesota-Duluth (public)
MS	University of Mississippi (public)

MT	University of Montana, Missoula (public)
NE	University of Nebraska-Lincoln (public)
ND	University of North Dakota (public)
CA	University of San Francisco
CA	University of the Pacific
OK	University of Tulsa
MO	Webster University

Axis 2 Liberal Arts Colleges

MI	Albion College
PA	Alleghany College (PA)
KY	Asbury College (KY)
WI	Beloit College
VT	Bennington College (VT)
GA	Berry College
MI	Calvin College
KY	Centre College
IA	Coe College
IA	Cornell College
IN	Earlham College
FL	Eckerd College
MA	Gordon College
MD	Goucher College
IN	Hanover College
AR	Hendrix College
MI	Hope College
NY	Houghton College
MI	Kalamazoo College
IL	Knox College
IL	Lake Forest College
CA	Loyola Marymount University
IA	Luther College
NY	Marist College
GA	Mercer University
CA	Mills College (women's)
MS	Millsaps College
NE	Nebraska Wesleyan University
OH	Ohio Wesleyan University
WI	Ripon College
FL	Rollins College

WI	Saint. Norbert College (WI)
IN	St. Mary's College (IN)
IN	Wabash College (men's)
IA	Wartburg College
PA	Washington & Jefferson College
MD	Washington College
OH	Wittenberg University

Axis 3 Private Liberal Arts Colleges

MI	Alma College
KY	Bellarmine University
KS	Bethel College
AL	Birmingham Southern College
TN	Carson-Newman College
IA	Central College
GA	Clark Atlanta University (HBCU)
ID	College of Idaho
IL	Columbia College-Chicago
NJ	Drew University
IL	Elmhurst College
MA	Emmanuel College
FL	Flagler College
KY	Georgetown College
VA	Hampton University (HBCU)
AR	Harding University
NE	Hastings College
IL	Illinois College
IN	Indiana Wesleyan University
AR	John Brown University
IL	Millikin University
IL	Monmouth College
NJ	Monmouth University
WI	Northland College
GA	Oglethorpe University
IA	Simpson College
GA	Spelman College (HBCU)
MA	Suffolk University
WV	West Virginia Wesleyan College
MO	Westminster College
CA	Westmont College
MO	William Jewell College

Test Optional Colleges

College	Mean GPA
Agnes Scott College (GA)	3.7
Bard College (NY)	3.5
Bates College (ME)	3.7
Bowdoin College (ME)	3.8
Brandeis University (MA)	3.8
Bryant University (RI)	3.4
Bryn Mawr College (PA)	3.7
Clark University (MA)	3.7
College of the Holy Cross (MA)	3.7
DePaul University (IL)	3.6
Earlham College (IN)	3.6
Fairfield University (CT)	3.4
Hampshire College (MA)	3.5
Hobart and William Smith (NY)	3.4
Hofstra University (NY)	3.6
Lewis and Clark College (OR)	3.9
Loyola University Maryland (MD)	3.5
Pitzer College (CA)	3.6
Providence College (RI)	3.4
Sarah Lawrence College (NY)	3.7
Smith College (MA)	3.7
St. Lawrence University (NY)	3.5
Union College (NY)	3.4
Wake Forest University (NC)	3.8
Washington University (MO)	3.7
Wesleyan University (CT)	3.8
Worcester Polytechnic Institute (MA)	3.7

GPA Indexed Colleges

California State University Campuses
www.csumentor.edu (search eligibility index)
    California Polytechnic State University-San Luis Obispo*
    San Diego State University*
    California Maritime Academy*
    California State University-Chico*
    California State University-Long Beach*
    Sonoma State University*
    California State University-Fullerton*
    California State University-Channel Islands*
    California State Polytechnic University-Pomona*
    California State University-Stanislaus
    California State University-Fresno
    California State University-Northridge
    San Francisco State University
    San Jose State University
    California State University-San Marcos
    California State University-San Bernardino
    California State University-Sacramento
    California State University-East Bay
    Humboldt State University
    California State University-Bakersfield
    California State University-Monterey Bay
    California State University-Los Angeles
    California State University-Dominguez Hills

indicates campuses with graduation rates above 50 percent

University System of Georgia
gacollege411.org (search: freshman index requirements)
    University of Georgia*
    Georgia Institute of Technology*
    Georgia College and State University*
    North Georgia College & State University*
    Georgia State University*
    Georgia Southern University*
    Kennesaw State University
    Valdosta State University
    Albany State University
    University of West Georgia
    Southern Polytechnic State University
    Columbus State University
    Savannah State University
    Armstrong Atlantic State University
    Fort Valley State University
    Georgia Southwestern State University
    Clayton State University
    Augusta State University

Colorado State University System
http://highered.colorado.gov (search: index score)
    University of Colorado at Boulder*
    Colorado State University*
    University of Colorado at Colorado Springs
    University of Colorado Denver

Iowa Regents
http://www.regents.iowa.gov/RAI/
    Iowa State University*
    University of Iowa*
    University of Northern Iowa*

---

indicates campuses with graduation rates above 50 percent

Western Kentucky University, KY *
https://www.wku.edu/admissions/cai.php

University of Oregon, OR *
https://admissions.uoregon.edu/apply/gpachart.htm

Utah State University, UT *
https://www.usu.edu/admissions/freshmen/apply

Central Washington University, WA *
https://www.cwu.edu/admissions/index-calculator

Alabama State University, AL
http://www.alasu.edu

Northern Arizona University, AZ
http://nau.edu/admissions

Fort Lewis College, CO
https://www.fortlewis.edu

Boise State University, ID
http://admissions.boisestate.edu/index/indexcurrent

Morehead State University, KY
http://www.moreheadstate.edu/Requirements/

Southern Utah University, UT
https://www.suu.edu/prostu/admissionindex.html

indicates campuses with graduation rates above 50 percent

CHAPTER 8

Fit Is Flavor

Choosing the right college is all about finding a school that is going to do well by you, and where you feel you can do well. The previous chapters laid out strategies to help you find a quality college and avoid colleges that don't have your best interests in mind. While finding a quality college is the foundation for college success, it is not the only ingredient that goes into a successful college experience. Selecting a college is a lot like buying a cake. We need the cake itself to be a quality product, but in addition to quality, we also need to consider flavor. In the realm of higher education, college flavor is referred to as *fit*. A college that feels welcoming and provides the opportunities that match our education and career goals is said to be a good fit. A college that does not feel welcoming to us and does not provide the opportunities we are looking for is said to not be a good fit. In this chapter, you will hear from two students with dramatically different experiences with the college search process. Think about the choices each student made in high school and how those choices impacted their college options—and later their college experiences.

MALIK
It Just Didn't Click

I wasn't one of those who were like the top of the class or anything like that. In our group, I was the athlete. I was the star athlete of the school and everything. So it was sports first and then education for me. My high school counselor always had to remind me that education comes first—before sports; participating in sports was a privilege. But, as she was telling me that, it didn't always click. I was like, "Yeah, whatever. It's just education. I'll get by on playing basketball in college." My priority needed to be focusing on college, but I didn't realize that until the end of my senior year. And then it hit, like, "Whoa, you didn't get enough scholarships!" So, as we started to pick colleges at the end of our senior year, I got two basketball scholarships, but they weren't giving me enough. It was like, "We'll give you ten percent of your tuition if you come play for us."—but the tuition was over thirty thousand. My counselor would just say, "You know, if you go here it's going to be expensive, and you need the grades to go here, because you have to keep up your academics to play."

I came out of high school with like a 2.6 or 2.7 GPA. My ACT wasn't the highest either. During the practice tests I ranged between a 19 and 22, but when I took the actual test I got an 18. Then I retook it and got a 19. So that's where my ACT and GPA were. As I started applying to more colleges, I started to get desperate, because a lot of what my counselor was telling me was starting to make sense. And I was like, "I don't want to go here if I'm going to fail out." And so, we started to narrow it down. We found Norford College, an affordable college in-state that none of the students had gone to or really heard of. At Norford College I would basically have had school paid for. After high school that's where I went. I got to Norford, and it was good for the most part. And then my grades started to slip and I wasn't able to play. I just didn't make the transition. I just didn't get that work has to come first. Then reality hit me, like, "I really can't play; what am I going to do?" Basketball was my everything.

In high school my teachers were always telling me to stay on top of things. But in college, no one does that; you are on your own. You have to learn how to prioritize, how to time manage. That was a big thing. I always put other things first before work, but it caught up. Eventually I got kicked out of Norford, but I was able to write a letter to get back into the school. My second year I was so far behind in my cumulative GPA that I still couldn't play basketball. I was kinda like, "Alright, I'll try and get my GPA up so I can play later in the year"—but that didn't really happen. I kinda got depressed because I couldn't play. Then I started to think about things back at home, because my father had passed, and I missed him. That had made me stronger in high school, but thinking about that now in college, I was just thinking, "I wish he was around to be someone to talk to. Maybe he could have changed things."

There was just a bunch of stuff that was happening—just growing up too fast. I was doing everything else other than school. I was partying and hanging out. And people would be hanging out with me, but then they would be like, "You should consider doing your work before you go anywhere." But, I was always like, "I'll do it later; I got time." It never clicked to me.

When I started at Norford they put me in sophomore classes because of my background in high school: a couple AP classes. They set me up with a whole Sophomore schedule when I was a freshman, and it was really, really hard—and I was failing. They put me in a macro-economics class that was like junior level. They just saw my transcript and thought I could handle it. They gave me a really, really hard schedule my first semester, and I had to work. My first job ever was campus security. When I was working campus security, I would work like 6pm-midnight. And then on the weekends I had to work all weekend, like 6pm-2am. I didn't get a day off. This was the first time I had a job, and I had to balance that and going to school—and basketball. It was really, really hard. At Norford you had to work. That was the only way you could attend that college. If you wanted to live on campus, you had to have a job on campus. It's a work college. If you lost your job, then you had to leave the school. There was none of this staying on campus and not having a job. You had to pack up and go home. At this school, people grew up in the town—went to elementary school in the town, went to high school in the town, went to college in the town, and taught in the town. That's how it was.

When things got rough, I got a letter in my mailbox saying I was going to be on academic probation if I didn't get it together. So I went to my counselor, and it was no help. The counseling there was horrible. It was so bad. They couldn't come up with an action plan for me. They didn't follow up or check on anybody. It was like if you had a problem, then you were just kinda left in the dark. They really didn't do a good job of breaking things down or telling me what classes I needed to take. They really didn't help me come up with a schedule that worked best for me, or even worked for me at all. To be honest, it just wasn't good. My high school counselors would have been twice as good. Don't get me wrong, the college works for some people, but it didn't work for me, and it seems like it didn't work for urban kids. The kids from the town—they were used to it. They had been working since high school because they had always been provided with jobs. You know, everybody knows everybody, so there was always a job. When you come from a city and go to high school in a city, most people don't have a job. I know for me, in high school, having a job wouldn't have been an option, because I didn't have transportation. I would have had to travel really far to find work; there wouldn't have been any time. With sports, I was in school basically like ten hours a day.

The school didn't know how to handle urban kids. I mean, it was equally hard for everyone, but some of the professors already knew the kids from the town, and so it was kinda harder for kids that weren't from around there. It's hard to build relationships because they're not seeking out those relationships with you. They did bring in an African American counselor. She eventually left, but for the semester that she was there, she really helped me. She worked with my high school counselor and they talked, and they had a good understanding. But then, after she left, things just started to break down. I just didn't have the knowledge, and I couldn't figure it out. I think another thing that was good was my high school counselor would talk to her *or email her and together they would figure out what was going on, and what I needed to do. When your high school counselor can connect with your college counselor that is always helpful.*

That first year is so crucial. You can get distracted as a freshman so easily, unless you have been training yourself in high school to get work done and not procrastinate. You're not in college to have fun. The main reason you're in college is for your education: to get that degree. My last semester I had there was my best semester. My semester GPA was really high, but my cumulative was still low. I didn't bring my cumulative back up above the threshold; I was like .2 points away. If I had brought my GPA up over that, I would have been eligible for financial aid the next semester, but I wasn't able to get my cumulative up that high. I lost my financial aid. The thing is, they didn't tell me I lost my financial aid until I got all the way back to campus. I went to go get my dorm key, and they said I had a red flag on my account and I couldn't get my key because I didn't have financial aid. They said, "We can give you your key and you can pay everything out of pocket, or you can go home." They ended up giving me a week. I sat in my dorm for a week. But when classes started, I had to be gone. My mom came down and got me and brought me home.

I had wanted to go to this other college out-of-state. Back in high school they were actively recruiting me to play basketball. I think I would have been way happier there because the school was just put together so much better. I feel like I would have had my troubles there, but I would have been more supported too. I couldn't go because it was like $11,000 out of pocket. At Norford it was only $3,000 out of pocket. Those were the two cheapest options I had. Most people fix things and get it together before their senior year in high school, but I was one of those people who didn't. After my experience at Norford I have so much more ambition. I take care of business first, like no other.

Success is a Two-Way Street

There are so many layers to Malik's story. On the surface is the story of a young man who didn't prioritize academics in high school and ended up with college options that were less than ideal. Just under that is the story of a young man who struggled with the transition to college and wasn't able to get on track in time to keep his scholarships. Then there is the layer of college fit. It seems that no matter what kind of student Malik had been, the "personality" of the school just did not fit him. Lastly, Malik's story is also one of institutional effectiveness. No matter which way you slice it, this college match was destined for a breakup. That's too bad, because Malik seems to have finally figured out how to perform to his academic abilities, and it seems that this small-town college really works for some students, just not Malik.

If we think back to when Malik was in high school, I am sure we could come up with some advice for him. It probably would sound a lot like the advice he was already getting. Malik sees that now, but it took some hard lessons to get there. Why? Why didn't Malik just start out high school focused on grades instead of sports? Why did it take until the end of his senior year before he realized the repercussions of putting fun before work? Malik, like a lot of students, had a difficult time imagining the long-term consequences of his choices. Focusing on the now instead of the future is called being *present-oriented*. We are all born present-oriented. Being present-oriented serves a really important function from an evolutionary standpoint. Resources were scarce for our distant ancestors, and so taking advantage of the opportunities in the present was important to survival. After all, who knew when the next meal was coming? Those of us who grew up with limited resources might have been forced to be present-oriented to get by. The problem is, long-term success requires us to be *future-oriented*.

School is a future-oriented activity. You have to decide to put the effort in today when you may not see the rewards of those efforts for years (or decades) to come. Sure, you get grades, but grades are just an abstract marker to show colleges and employers down the road how successful you were in school. An A doesn't feed you today, but the accumulation of As might very well effect how well you eat later in life. Making future-oriented decisions is not a skill that most teenagers have fully developed yet. Sometimes it takes a big loss before such an abstract concept really hits home. For Malik, this didn't happen until the end of his senior year, leaving him with very few affordable college options. Malik may have been able to get into a variety of colleges, but without the grades, he just couldn't compete for the scholarships that could have made these schools affordable.

Even though Malik states that prioritizing sports over academics in high school wasn't the best idea, his behavior didn't change much in college. Why? Malik takes responsibility for his choices, pointing out that he should have prioritized work over fun. But, he also states that he didn't know how to manage his time, and that he struggled with handling work, classes, and a social life. Malik lacked some very basic study skills and time management skills that limited his ability to be successful in college. As a high school student, you might not have someone at your school dedicated to helping you improve your study skills or time management skills, but colleges do. These services are usually found in the academic services or student services department at your school. If you don't know what services are available, you can do some looking online, approach one of your professors, or ask someone who looks like they have been on campus for a while. There is absolutely nothing embarrassing about stopping a random person on campus and asking a question. It might feel weird, but it's not. At the end of the day, your academic success is far more important than your ego.

Then there is the issue of *fit*. Fit is a funny term to use when talking about a college, but it means pretty much the same thing in education as it does in fashion. Some colleges look amazing online, but once you try them on they just don't feel right: they don't fit. Based on what Malik shared, it doesn't seem like this college fit him very well. First of all, the work component of the college was really new to Malik. Growing up in Chicago, it was not common for people in Malik's network to work in high school. Finding a job without work experience can be difficult, and the jobs Malik could find would have required him to commute long distances, which would have eliminated his ability to play sports. So Malik showed up to a work college with no work experience. This could have been a great learning experience for Malik, but balancing work and school while lacking strong study skills and time management skills was just too much for him to overcome. Add an inattentive college to the mix, and Malik's struggles became insurmountable.

BREAK IT DOWN

Malik

- *What do you think is the moral of Malik's story?*
- *Why did Malik have to come home?*
- *What events happened that led to Malik's leaving school?*
- *Is there anything Malik could have done differently in college to change the outcome of his story?*
- *Is there anything that Malik could have done differently back in high school to change the outcome of his story?*

CHAPTER 9

You Are More Than a Number

How are you feeling? No really, how are you feeling so far? Have you noticed yourself getting discouraged? What about angry? Have you wanted to throw this book across the room yet? Do you know why? Could it be that I am trying to reduce you—this wholly unique and beautiful person—down to a GPA and test score, and use those to determine the rest of your entire life? Yeah. I get it. Here we are on Chapter Nine and almost everything we have gone over so far boils down to numbers: GPA, ACT/SAT, Axis, graduation rate, scholarships, etc. Where are you in this process? When do you get to be more than a set of numbers? I want to make something incredibly clear: you are so much more than a set of numbers, and your grades and test scores do not define you as a person, not now and not ever. But, that doesn't mean we should approach the college admissions process empty handed.

Back in Chapter Two I mentioned cultivating your inner ninja. Well, admissions criteria is a prime opportunity to do just that. Colleges are actively using grades and test scores to make decisions about your admissions, whether we like it or not. Instead of running from this reality, we can take possession of it and use it to your advantage. That's being a college-going ninja. Colleges may make the admissions decisions, but they have no control over where you apply. The reality is, you have the tactical advantage. You have a plethora of information bout yourself and the colleges you are considering. We can use this advantage to help craft a good college application list that will boost your chances of getting accepted. That's the data part. Once you have decided where you want to apply, you walk away from the numbers and focus on presenting yourself as a whole candidate to the admissions team. You do this through your admissions essays and short answer questions on the application. We'll cover this more in Section 3.

Even though much of the college application process is focused on numbers, you still have many opportunities to engage your potential colleges as a whole candidate, even before you apply. College visits, college fairs, and college rep visits are fantastic ways for you to get to know colleges and let them get to know you. In this Chapter, you will hear from Jasmine, a bright and determined student who started off her college search process feeling limited by her finances, grades and test scores. Despite her hesitation, Jasmine remained focused on getting to know each college personally before she applied, and eventually landed herself a great college.

JASMINE
Put Yourself Out There

For me, it really came down to the money, because I don't come from a wealthy family. It was spring when Grenier University flew me out for free. I didn't really think a school would fly me out for free, but I thought, "Well, let's just go to Ohio and see what it's about." I had already been to visit Luther two times, and I had visited Monmouth and Northern Illinois. I had been to the University of Texas, Austin to study over the summer, and we had been to Georgetown with the law club. We also visited places like Notre Dame, but when I visited Grenier, I was like, "Wow, I want to go here."

My entire high school career numbers always brought me down. It was always like your ACT, your grades, your GPA, and I wasn't close to the top of my class, so I didn't even apply to my top choice—the University of Wisconsin, Madison—because I *didn't think I'd get in, or get a lot of financial aid. The numbers always brought me down, but for some reason I applied to Grenier anyway. Then I visited Grenier. I visited a lot of classrooms, and the school really caught my attention. I knew I wanted small classes so I could get a lot more personal attention and have a more personal relationship with the professors. When I think about it now, Grenier was one of the most expensive schools I applied to, but I am only paying like $2,000 a semester because they offered me a good scholarship; they helped me a lot.*

I knew I wanted to get an education. No doubt about it. Many of my teachers in high school still had college loans, so I was like, "I'm not going to get away from loans." The price is always going to be there. I just thought about it, put my feet on the ground, and took a look at my position in life. Other people don't have this opportunity, and I shouldn't let a few numbers define me. Going to Grenier and getting this great education is worth being a few thousand dollars in debt in the future.

I did cry my first day at Grenier because I was going to miss my family, but I just opened my door and started talking to people. I also did this orientation thing where we visited DC with other freshmen, and we did service there a week before school started. There were a few other girls on my floor that were in DC too, and so I opened my door and I was just like fixing my stuff. Then some of them came by; we ordered pizza and then started talking. I guess that made me feel better. Before, I was just like, "Right now I am in this room alone and crying; I need to get over it. I am going to be here for a year, so I need to get over it." The next day, we started the actual program, and I felt better. Not once did I question why I was at Grenier. Sometimes I would question myself, when I was lazy in class or didn't want to get up. Then I would think, "I'm getting this scholarship to be here, so get up." It was a motivator.

At Grenier you really need to get to know your professors to see if they can open up opportunities for research or internships in the summer. My freshmen year I wasn't really thinking about that. I had classes, so I spoke to my professors sometimes, but *not really a deep kind of connection. I kinda feel like I lost a year of college because I didn't take advantage of all the opportunities that Grenier offered. But sophomore year I started going to my professors' office hours; I emailed them if I had questions; I posed questions in class just so they knew I was reading the articles and thinking about what they were teaching us. Also, one thing I started doing sophomore year was going to the Career Exploration Office, and they helped me with my resume. I literally went there like twenty times last year—not only for my resume, but for internships over the summer. They helped me find scholarships and things that other people didn't know about. Without them I don't know what I would have done. I got a $3,300 scholarship to do an internship this summer, so I am going to Costa Rica for journalism and media.*

Going into college I didn't think about how I was going to be one of the few minorities in school. It is one of those things you don't see on the website; you have to experience it. So when I first realized that, when I went to classes and stuff, I was just overwhelmed. In high school there was like only one white person in our class; I was surrounded by Hispanics and African Americans. So it was a shock to go to college and be surrounded by the people that I wasn't surrounded by before. I was worried that they were going to have these judgments of me. You have this idea in your head that these people are mean and stuff like that. At the beginning I was only with my group of friends. I didn't really go out and defeat stereotypes and let people know I'm not "this way"—I'm a human being just like you. By the end of freshmen year I had realized that I was just holding myself back. I decided I should just take a step forward and try to interact, and not let the stuff I'd heard get in the way of me being friends with someone. My sophomore year was better. I guess I just realized that everyone is the same—that everybody has these things in their heads that are instilled in them and you just have to go out of your way and take the initiative to get to know people.

I soon realized that I didn't really get the education that I had wanted growing up. I mean, other people at Grenier went to like boarding schools or private schools. They were faster than me, and they knew more than me, and at one point I felt like I wasn't ready or wasn't meant to be in these classrooms because they already knew things that I didn't know. But then I realized that everyone learns at a different pace, and everyone has different experiences.

When I was in high school I used to think I was going to go to college and get a job, because I thought that was the only option. But after actually going to college and talking to people and seeing what alumni are doing, now I see my future as continuing my education, and that was something I never considered because of money. Now, I want to do a Master's program and join the Peace Corps. I'm a person that likes to have options. My goal now is not to get a job right away but to try and do other things to get more experience.

A Case for Playing the Field

When it comes to picking a college, I strongly recommend you keep it neutral until March or April of your senior year. No matter how appealing, don't get stuck on one or two colleges without seeing what's out there first. You may end up attending the same college you've been set on since freshman year, but chances are you won't. Why? Because colleges (and people) look much more appealing when you don't have anything to compare them to. Jasmine's story is a strong case for getting out there and seeing colleges early in your high school career. Would Jasmine have ended up at Grenier if she hadn't gone and visited? Probably not.

Jasmine took the time to learn what she liked and didn't like by visiting a wide range of schools as early as her freshmen year in high school. However, not all of us have access to the college trips that Jasmine was lucky enough to go on in her early years of high school. If you find getting onto college campuses difficult early in your college search, you can still benefit immensely by attending national, state, city-wide, district-wide, or high school college fairs.

You should aim to attend your first college fair sometime during your freshman or sophomore year of high school. College fairs are the 'speed dating' of higher education, and there is no better way to shake the nervousness of talking to potential colleges than in a sea of unknown faces where time is short and memories are shorter. If you are able to make it to a large fair, you could easily talk to over thirty college reps in one visit. The first few reps you talk to might leave your palms sweaty and your heart racing, but by college number three you will begin to find your stride. The key to getting the most out of a college fair is to do some self-reflection ahead of time. You don't need to go into a fair with your future planned out. However, you do want to have some key information on hand to address common questions the reps might ask, and to help you feel more comfortable engaging in conversations with people you've only just met.

In Section Three you will find brainstorming exercises to help you prepare to talk to college reps.

Once you've pursued the college fair scene, you are ready to visit actual colleges. Visit lots of colleges, and I'm not talking about surfing the web. I'm talking about plunking your feet down on actual soil. College websites show you the best of the best they have to offer, not what a typical student experiences on a day-to-day basis. I've seen teeny-tiny colleges in the middle of nowhere present themselves like giant flagship universities on their website. I've seen the most dull-drum commuter schools fill their homepage with colorful images of young people living it up in the city. Sad. It's just sad. These schools are hoping that you will be one of the many, many students out there who are online shoppers. It's much easier to put on the appearance of being an amazing school than to actually be one. Don't fall for it.

By your junior year you should be hitting the college pavement. Visit a large research university. Visit a local commuter school. Visit a liberal arts college. Visit a private faith-based school. Visit a private secular school. Take a look around. Put on your critical thinking hat and pretend you are looking at colleges for someone else, like a younger sibling. Ask questions. Are students assigned a particular advisor? How often do students meet with their advisor? Is there a multi-cultural student union on campus? Do they offer advising as well? What opportunities exist on campus for research experience, faculty mentorship, or on-campus work experience? If you start visiting different types of colleges early in your high school career it will be much easier as a senior to tell if a college should end up on your list of possible schools.

Your sophomore and junior years are the ideal time to visit local colleges and gain some general knowledge about what different types of colleges look and feel like. If a school is local, take time during the week to see what the school's campus life is really like. Don't go when the school is on break. Try not to go in the dead of winter. And, most importantly, don't go on a weekend! You want to see the campus as close to how you can expect to experience it if you were actually to attend school there. Yes, this might mean getting out of school early to take a campus tour or taking a day or two off to visit a school further away. Work with your teachers, advisor, and counselor early in the year to schedule these dates. It's okay to go with friends; just make sure they aren't going to goof off or distract you. You want to enjoy yourself, but you also want to make a good impression.

Once you are a senior, you will need to visit the actual colleges you are considering attending. You should make every effort to visit the top five schools you have been accepted to. Visiting colleges may require planning a series of day trips or an overnight trip. Don't go alone unless you are participating in a fly-out program. If your family isn't able to accompany you, get together with some classmates that have their heads on straight and see if one of their parents is able to go with the group. Plan to visit a few different campuses. Make sure you involve the adults in your life in the planning. Get their feedback. Make it a big deal. Share your plans with relatives long before the trip. If money is tight, ask if people can contribute to your college trip instead of buying you birthday or holiday gifts. Do a budget. Be reasonable with money, and plan ahead.

It might sound harsh, but I'm going to tell you something I have told many of my students: if you can't find the time, spend the money, or figure out the logistics of visiting the campus now, how do you expect to get there in the fall? Look, I know life can present serious obstacles to visiting a potential college, especially for those of us without a lot of money. But we either need to dig in and find a way to make it work, or we need to be realistic about the level of challenge these obstacles are going to pose for us in the future.

If you have a solid GPA, there are ways to get to campuses for free (or next to free). Some liberal-arts schools will provide travel for highly-qualified students. If you can't afford to pay for travel costs, ask the schools you are considering if they have travel scholarships or fly-out programs. If you are a low-income student, such programs serve as a strong sign that the school will be understanding of your financial situation once you are on campus as well. Things change every year, but you can find a list of schools that have offered fly-out opportunities in the past in Section 3.

BREAK IT DOWN
Jasmine

- How did visiting colleges in high school impact where Jasmine ultimately decided to go to college?
- Is Jasmine satisfied with her college experience?
- Do you think she would have been just as satisfied anywhere she went?
- What college fairs do you have access to at school or in your city?

You don't have to go far to find happiness, but maybe you should. Maybe you hate your hometown. Maybe you are taken with the image of New England fall colors. Maybe you are just looking for the chance to move where no one knows you—someplace where you can reinvent yourself into someone completely different from who you are right now. These are all perfectly reasonable motivators to expand your college search to the ends of the continent (and beyond if you like). I would just offer you a word of advice before you start calculating how much money you are going to need to book a plane ticket home for the holidays. When selecting a college, distance can be an enormous asset (especially if you have distractions at home that require a great deal of your time or energy). However, distance can also pose some significant challenges (like having to build an entirely new network of supports away from anything and everyone you have ever known). Instead of focusing on how far from home a school is, focus on what the college has to offer you in meeting your educational and personal growth goals.

Attending a college where most of the students commute to school is a really different experience than going away to college. Keep in mind that college is about so much more than earning a degree. For most of us, college is our last experience with formal education. Think of yourself like play-dough, and each year of school as a different process that shapes the dough. What do you want your last few years of schooling to shape you into? When you go away to school you are dedicating 100% of your time to shaping yourself into the adult you will be for the rest of your life. Going away to college is like adulthood with training wheels. You get to practice making decisions, negotiating relationships, and trying on different versions of yourself. And you know the best part? You get to make mistakes and grow without the critical eye of the adult world. That's an opportunity you will never get again in your life. It's a one-time offer. Miss the boat, and there won't be another one.

While I am a huge advocate for going away to school if it is possible, I know that going away to college is not an option for everyone. If you do not get a financial aid package that makes going away to school financially possible, then you are going to have to figure out which school is going to offer you the best education for your money close to home. Many commuter schools struggle to foster the same sense of community as residential schools. However, there are some really good gems out there that succeed in providing supports for commuter students both academically and socially. So, how can you identify schools that support commuter students? With the same tool you have already been using: graduation rate. This time, though, we are going to throw in one more statistic: commuter status. If a college is predominantly a commuter school, and still has a solid graduation rate, they must be doing something right. Whether you ultimately choose to go away for college or stay close to home, don't write either one off in the early phases of your research. Keep an open mind. You never know what opportunities (and obstacles) are going to present themselves in the end.

SECTION 2

SUCCEEDING IN COLLEGE

Introduction

I hear a lot of students and families talk about their students "going" to college, but going to college is not enough. Getting into college is an enormous accomplishment, but it is only the first step in a much longer journey. Instead, we need to talk about "graduating" from college. Focusing on "going" to college frames college acceptance as the reward for working hard in high school. While your preparation in high school qualifies you for the college race, it's not the race itself. To graduate from college you are going to need to stay academically on top of your game, until you finally cross that finish line. This doesn't mean you can't make mistakes. Everyone makes mistakes, and everyone struggles at some point in college. However, how you respond to these struggles and what steps you take to ensure you get back on track are what really count.

In the next few chapters we are going to hear from students who faced unforeseen challenges in college. While you are reading their stories think about the choices these students made.

- What choices were beneficial?

- What choices had negative consequences?

- Would you have done anything differently if you were in their shoes?

CHAPTER 10

The Many Colors of Racism

Conversations about racism usually focus on acute and egregious instances of racism. But racism is not always overt, and racism wears many dispositions and intentions. Sometimes institutions and individuals with the best intentions can do irreparable harm. If you are a person of color, or someone who identifies with a marginalized group, you will undoubtedly experience some form of acute or systemic discrimination while in college. How you interpret, respond, and are affected by these events largely depends on the reactions and responses of the community around you. In this chapter you will hear from two students who were confronted with both acute and institutional racism while away at college, and their experiences couldn't be more different. As you are reading, reflect on each student's experience and how it aligns or diverges with your own experiences of racism, or from what you have been taught to identify as racism.

AUBREY

Expected to Fail

College wasn't really pushed in my household. My parents never went, and I lived mostly with my mom, and she wasn't really around. I mean, she was there for us, but my brother and I mostly did our own thing. I would do my school work because...well, I have really bad anxiety, and I was just afraid of being in trouble with my mom, and I could do the work, so I just did it. That was my mentality through high school. Later I started getting presentations from the high school staff promoting college, and how college could increase your income. Really, I just wanted to go to college to get away from home. I really just wanted to get out of the state; I did not care about increasing my income. That's why I applied to schools mostly out of state like Culpepper College, and a few Ivy League schools. I had a lot of confidence, and I wanted to do the best that I could.

Honestly, my high school college counselor was a big part of my decision making in where to go to college. She was there to help me apply for the fly-out program to visit Culpepper. That kinda got me excited. It showed me what college could be like, what it was like to be in another state, the opportunities I could have, etc. So, when I got waitlisted for Culpepper I got discouraged and thought, "Well, I'm just going to have to stay in state." I was deeply disappointed because I didn't want to stay in state. Again, she stepped in and really encouraged me. I am glad that I took her advice and sent back the waitlist form to Culpepper, because they offered me a good scholarship. So, that was the precursor in my journey to college.

When I got to Culpepper, I started to feel a lack of motivation. At first, it was a deep sigh of relief: I had just finished high school, and that was a lot of homework. I don't know what I expected, because in my mind I was like, "Yeah, I'm going to college and I have to do work"—but I didn't really care that much. I don't know exactly. There was something in me that was nonchalant. I lost my motivation. I wasn't near my mom anymore, and I wasn't running away from that anymore. So, when I first got to Culpepper they invited a few of the minority students to a bridge program, to help us get the feel of college. They anticipated that we would have a little more problem acclimating because we were minority students. In the bridge program, I really didn't do homework. I felt like I wasn't working to the best of my ability. So, the professors I had... I just felt like they weren't confident in my skill level or my ability to perform in college. That kind of made me anxious. I was like, "I can definitely do the work here," but somehow I just could not bring myself to feel motivated.

I did end up getting severely depressed in college. I could not even go to class. I had such anxiety. Every time I would sit in class, I would try and talk, but the words just would not come out. I would just shake, and think, "I can't do this." But I kept forcing myself to stay because I knew that I could do it. I kept thinking, "You do want to do this; a degree will help you. You do want to become a first-generation college graduate." That's what I just kept telling myself in the back of my head. I sought out counseling sessions on campus. I was trying to take advantage of counseling, to dissect the situation, and see what I needed to do to move forward. But, I wasn't really discovering anything that I didn't know already. It felt like there was something more.

What I really felt was cheated. When I would write papers in college, I would write papers in like six hours and get a "C," but that would be without reading any of the material. When I would go to class and hand it in to the professor, I was too afraid to admit that I didn't do any of the reading, and that I was still able to write the paper. In the professor's mind... he thought it was a lack of skill. But I wanted to tell him, "No, I am very smart." I started to feel inadequate, like I couldn't be at Culpepper—like I was only there because of Affirmative Action.

Racism on college campuses is extremely prevalent. Me, I don't experience micro-aggressions on a daily basis, because I do pass for white. But people I associated with in The Black Student Union, or the Native American Student Union, those students experience micro-aggressions daily. I just started to feel more uncomfortable being at Culpepper. It started as a lack of motivation and an inability to put in a lot of effort, and slowly progressed into feeling like an unhealthy environment. It seems like diversity was promoted, but more so in the brochure than in the dorms.

I think my professor did try and understand. I don't think it was so much racially motivated, but rather my socio-economic background, and him knowing I was from Chicago. As soon as I said I was from Chicago, I swear everyone thought I had a gun in my bag. I'm like, "Are you kidding me?" I remember talking to my professor about my struggles and him giving me this example of a study that was done with writers: they were given material that they were unfamiliar with, and because of the lack of familiarity, they couldn't really write to the best of their ability. He was trying to be understanding, but... I was crying and sobbing during the meeting and he was just cringing. I felt even more uncomfortable. Then I had to speak with the Dean. I felt like it was such a high stress situation having to meet one-on-one with the Dean. She kept asking me if I wanted to go to some other college, and I thought, "If I wanted to go to another college, I would have gone there in the first place. I traveled here with pennies, and I am trying to get a good education at one of the top liberal arts schools, and you are trying to push me off to some lower-tiered school?" Not that other schools were bad school, but come on. There are tiers, let's be honest. That was my freshman year, first semester.

I kept taking philosophy courses, still trying to make it work, still feeling depressed. It was really hard to interact with the other students. I mean, I was in class with sons and daughters of CEOs. My parents don't even make $17,000 a year. It's not that I can't talk to them about anything, but they don't want to talk about the things I want to talk about. It felt like I was putting a puzzle piece...like I'm jamming it into a puzzle, and it obviously doesn't work. I mean, I loved going to class and listening to them talk. These kids were amazingly smart. I felt like I could do that...I could respond too, if I could just cough out the words. I just needed some support. It's not like I wasn't trying. Every time I would open my mouth to say something, it felt like swallowing water, like I was drowning again.

I came back for my sophomore year. I thought, "All right, let's try this again." But I dropped right away. I just felt like I was in a cloud. I felt so disconnected. I could not relate to my peers at all. In the middle of the year, I got a bill for about $2,000 for *miscellaneous charges, and they wanted me to pay that before I came back for spring semester. I thought, "I'm not paying you for a bad experience." So, when I got that bill, I packed up my things. I was kind of excited, because now I had a reason to say that I didn't quit: that I had to leave. So, I came back home.*

For a long time I thought I was going back to Culpepper. I was set on paying the bill off and getting back there. But then I realized I cannot go backwards. I can't go back to something that doesn't work. I tried twice. It just wasn't working. I started paying off that tuition bill last fall, and now I am down to about $680. I am going to go to a community college.

Race, Power, and Privilege

Sometimes, colleges with the best intentions can wreak considerable damage upon their students. Aubrey went into college a brilliant but anxious young woman, but left college emotionally distraught and questioning everything she thought she knew about herself: who she was, where she came from, and where she was going. Aubrey's college experience wasn't just fruitless, it was downright harmful. There is a lot more to Aubrey's story that I cannot share here in this book. However, I can tell you the emotional destruction that Aubrey endured rippled through every aspect of her life and her identity. Aubrey lost herself, and in that she lost everything.

Aubrey's college thought they were being proactive in connecting her to resources that they thought she needed. But what was the criteria that they used to determine if Aubrey needed help? What kind of help did they give her? Aubrey's downward spiral started the moment the college assumed her struggles were related to being an under-represented and a low-income student. Specifically, the college used Aubrey's ethnicity and socio-economic status as indicators that she wasn't academically prepared to keep up with her more affluent peers. By targeting only students of color for the bridge program, the college sent a very specific message: students of color are not expected to be successful here. Whether the college was welcoming to students of color actually becomes irrelevant. I can welcome you into my home, but if I seat you at a different table than the rest of my guests, I am sending a very clear message about where you belong in the group.

There is no doubt that Aubrey needed help. What she needed was a swift kick in the pants, and a mentor to check in with her weekly to ensure she was staying on top of her reading and being proactive with her papers. Aubrey was just being a slacker. The response from the school should have been to raise the bar, not lower it. Aubrey needed to hear, "You are at one of the top liberal arts schools in the country; you need to start acting like it"—not "We expect that you will struggle; minority students often have a hard time." The college's message was devastating to Aubrey because it turned a struggle that Aubrey saw as situational (lacking motivation) and presented it as something permanent (the result of her ethnicity and socio-economic background). She began to wonder if she really was smart enough to be there. She began to wonder if she was capable of being successful at the school. She began to feel like the only reason she had been admitted was because of her race/ethnicity. Slowly over time, Aubrey lost her own narrative and adopted the narrative the school provided her with.

The most devastating reality of Aubrey's story is that her outcome was not inevitable. The school could have done a much better job of putting individual students first, and recognizing the diverse range of experiences and abilities of their students—including students of color. Aubrey could have made some different decisions too. Aubrey was quick to tell me that she thinks if she had started off college putting forth her full effort, she would have excelled academically and would be well on her way to graduation. I want to point out that while this is probably true, it is also widely unfair. In essence, Aubrey is saying she could have circumvented the school's stereotype if only she had defied those stereotypes preemptively. That is whole-heartedly unfair, but it is also probably true.

Coming from a high school that was almost exclusively comprised of students of color, I am not sure that Aubrey was prepared to encounter the kind of institutionalized racism she experienced at Culpepper. I am not saying that Aubrey had been sheltered from racism before getting to college—quite the opposite. I am saying that Aubrey's experiences with racism were probably much more overt and clearly identifiable. The racism that Aubrey experienced at college was much more subtle and much more damaging than any racial slur. Aubrey received a daily dose of disempowerment, served to her on a silver platter by the very people who were supposed to be helping her. In the end, Aubrey did what she needed to do to protect herself: she left.

I wish I could say that Aubrey's school is the only college in America where you would encounter such an experience, but that just isn't the case. Privileged people and privileged institutions can do a lot of damage, even if they are motivated by good intentions. The root of this damage is not ignorance but the misuse of power. Aubrey was struggling with a lack of motivation that had more to do with being a teenager than it did ethnicity or socio-economic status. But, because the institution held the power in their relationship, they could rewrite Aubrey's personal history in a way that fit their expectations, regardless of whether it fit Aubrey's reality. A student with more social capital—with parents who paid full tuition, and therefore had financial influence over the school—would never have been treated the way Aubrey was.

Aubrey's experience is not representative of what every student of color experiences in college, but it is also not an anomaly. The reality is, if you are a student of color, a low-income student, or a first-generation college student, you will probably encounter some incarnation of what Aubrey experienced—if not in college then out in the work force. You need to have a plan beforehand for how you will engage institutions that threaten your sense of self. Maintaining relationships with healthy individuals from your past can be an immense source of strength and clarity. Maintaining these relationships is one reason why students find living at home and commuting to school so appealing. But, you do not need to live at home to maintain a strong sense of self. Sometimes going away does more for cementing your identity than living at home ever could. Building a social network that reflects your identity should be a high priority when you arrive at school, right behind getting your academic performance in check. If you are an underrepresented student at an elite college or university, socializing is not a luxury; it is a necessity for success. Just don't let it get too out of hand.

BREAK IT DOWN
Aubrey

- What do you think about Aubrey's story?
- What evidence is there that Aubrey faced racism at her college?
- What would you do if you were in her shoes?
- What advice would you give to a student or classmate who was experiencing racism on campus?
- Would it make a difference if the racism came from an individual (like calling someone a racial slur) or more institutional (like what Aubrey experienced)?

DOMINIQUE

The Importance of Family

When I visited Siskwell University, it was totally different than all the other visits to other colleges. When I walked on campus, it felt like home. It made me happy. Just walking across the quad I felt like I could get around on my own. I didn't need a map to tell me where to go. It was like I instantly knew the buildings. I knew the campus. I started meeting the people on campus. I feel like everybody has a certain school that they connect to more. I didn't really pay attention to the price tag of the school, like how much tuition would be. Being a first generation college student, I see a lot of people only pay attention to how much the school is. My mom was against me going to Siskwell, because it was $50,000.00 each year. But, I had faith, and my grandmother had faith, that if I wanted to go here I would make a way.

I actually got my acceptance letter on my birthday. I knew it was just meant to be. When I came to Siskwell it was different: I was finally on my own, doing my own thing. I didn't have my parents controlling my moves. The school was actually two hours away from my parents. Living in a dorm the first year was actually great. It taught me responsibility. But even more, it helped me grow as a person. I started to make even more decisions on my own. I realized the decisions I made could either benefit me or not benefit me. I was branching off and becoming my own person.

During my first year, some of my friends had problems with other students. We realized that some of the students… they didn't accept us being here. For example, a friend of mine, she was Black and she had a White roommate. Her roommate started making comments, like telling her mom she didn't want to be in that room and she didn't know why they would put them in the same room. She didn't like us to come by the room *or anything like that. She complained to her mother, and her mother called the school; it became a big problem. I didn't really understand why it happened until last semester.*

Last semester our school started to address situations like that. They asked us questions like, 'Personally, do you feel like you're not welcomed?' But I always did feel welcomed. I felt it was just one situation in which a girl may never have been surrounded by different races in her school or neighborhood, and it was a shock to her to have to share a room with someone who was not the same race as her. The girl ended up moving out of the room. One student actually wrote an article about the incident and said racial differences shouldn't be a problem for anyone, and that everyone should feel welcome. I felt that was a good step in trying to address the situation. My friend may have wanted it to be dealt with in a different way. But, I felt like it was dealt with in the best way that they could.

During this last year, we've grown so much. I think it's because our campus has acknowledged that racism still happens. Each class addressed it and tried to educate people who may not have acknowledged it before. When young African-American boys were killed by police officers, the black student union actually held open discussions on campus, and everybody was welcomed. They also invited the president of the campus, the students, and the deans. At the end of last semester there was also an incident where somebody had put a racial slur by our fountain. It was one of the carnival nights, and at about ten o'clock one of our African American students, a young lady, one of my friends, was walking back to her room. She saw it in chalk.

It prompted some conversations. The president sent out emails to all the students saying this is unacceptable and they would be looking into it, and that they were sorry and they couldn't understand why anyone would feel the need to write that. It was so crazy to actually have that happen on campus. That was addressed in a lot of our classrooms. I think a lot of the teachers just wanted to educate or just bring awareness about what was said. Our school tends to try to address issues as they occur to the best of their ability. There was actually an article about it in the newspaper. This town is little, so when something happens everybody knows about it.

Every school experience is different for every person. I believe every student who is figuring out their college process should make sure they feel like they will be welcomed into the campus. I would stay, visit, and have lunch with people on campus, and ask questions. I probably visited this school about twelve times before I came here. When some people ask how long I have been at Siskwell, I say I feel like I've been here eight years, because I fell in love with the school long before I came here.

I love all my professors. All of them make time to know every student. I can walk on campus and a professor will know my name. That's why I picked this school. Some of the schools I originally visited, the campuses were so big I felt like you might only get to know one or two professors out of your whole four years. But I can pass a professor I had in my Freshman year and they'll ask me how I am doing, how my classes are going.

In my sophomore year—close to the end of my semester—my grandmother passed away. I would say all my professors made me feel even more welcomed by checking up on me. I had plenty of friends that made me feel welcome also. Then, last year my daddy got killed. It happened in the final week when I came back to school. I had counseling all year. I had been, and still am, going to the trial for the murder. I would drive to Chicago and then go with my family to every trial. I've had the support of all my teachers. Last semester the trial was all semester, but I didn't fall behind. If I had to miss, my professors worked with me. They would send me the Power Points for that day, or if there was a quiz on that day my professors allowed me take it before or after depending on whether I felt prepared. A lot of my professors worked with me. Even before school started, one of my professors from last semester reached out to me and asked me how I was doing and let me know he was thinking *about me. It was hard times. He just wanted to see how the trial was going.*

I've learned to be much stronger since I've been away at college. I get so angry when I go to court. I try to control it, but my mind is so angry. My counselor told me it's because I didn't have time to grieve. I buried my dad two days before my birthday. It can be hard sometimes. I have days where I don't want to get out of bed, but I can't stay in the house. So I work. I go to school. I have some great friends; they support me. I tend to go to the library often. That way I get my work done instead of staying in bed. If I stay in the house for too long, then I start thinking, and I could have a breakdown. It's sometimes hard to talk with my mom, my auntie, or my sisters because I know they're going through stuff as well. Every time I go home for trial, I go to the cemetery. I spend around an hour, sometimes longer. I'll do like picnics at the cemetery. I'll visit my grandmother's grave for the first half. Then I go visit my dad's grave for the second half because they're both at the same cemetery: they're not too far from each other.

Sometimes I don't like to go home because it's not safe. When I go home I rent a car, because I don't like getting on the train or the bus. Being at Siskwell for four years, it's totally different from home. When I go home, people are fighting and stuff. I have not seen that once since I've been away at college. So when I go home, and I see something, I'm like, "What is going on?" I don't feel safe.

I want to own my own daycare. I would like to run a daycare in a house. A lot of kids in Chicago don't get the feeling of living in a home. We live in apartments. We live in certain neighborhoods, and we only see people in that neighborhood. Once we finally get in high school, we move a little farther from our neighborhood, but not too far. Some of my friends that I went to elementary school with should be graduating college with me. I feel like they should be on the same path as me. But, they're not, because they went to the neighborhood school that was up a block or two from us. I feel like they didn't have the teachers that I had in high school to push them, help them take the next step to move from that neighborhood farther out. When I talk to people I tell them, "Go to a college prep school; use it, because I don't want you to end up like the people in our neighborhood. You should not be doing the same thing you were doing when I went off to college."

You don't have to know everybody before you get to school, because you'll meet new friends. Don't give up. There's always help. Don't fear reaching out and asking for help; there is so much help available on campus. I feel like you'll develop a family outside of your family away at college. I know I've developed a family. My job at the cafeteria on campus—I've been here four years—I can say that's a family right there. I can say my friends who I met in college my freshman year are like family to me. We can have Sunday dinner together. I can call them over, and we'll do dinner; we'll pray and bless the food. Then we can have conversation and hang out. That's something I'd do if I were at home with my family.

An Extended Family

The deaths of Dominique's grandmother and father were not the first hardships she had ever known in life. Despite these challenges, Dominique has somehow found the peace, grace, and strength needed to finish college in the face of insurmountable hardship. Most certainly, Dominique's family and her faith have been enormous sources of strength for her; but so too has her school community. When I hear Dominique's story, I can't help but wonder what would have happened if Dominique had attended a different college. Would she have received the same support from her professors? Would she have developed the same kind of friendships? I am not sure. There is little doubt that Dominique loves her school, and I am eternally thankful that she was able to find a school family that provided her with the support she needed when times were rough. Even so, it would be dismissive to ignore that

Dominique and her friends experienced multiple instances of blatant racism on campus. I feel so unsettled when I think about how supportive the college community was of Dominique, and yet how ignorantly certain individuals on the college campus behaved. During our interview, I really tried to tease apart whether the events that Dominique described were the behaviors of a few students, or representative of an educational climate as a whole. Does it matter? Either way Dominique experienced hostile and discriminatory acts because of her race. Yes, it does matter.

An important part of college (and life) is being exposed to people from a wide variety of backgrounds. Unfortunately some of those individuals are going to be downright ignorant about people of different racial, ethnic, religious, language, gender identity, sexual orientation, or socio-economic backgrounds. These people, because of their privileged status, ignorance, or fear, might behave in a hostile manner towards you or your friends. If this happens, the school has an enormous responsibility to educate and set clear standards of behavior for the student body as a whole. I am not sure if the school responded in the most appropriate manner; what matters is not my opinion, but the fact that the school's response felt satisfactory for Dominique. Thus, Dominique was able to maintain a healthy sense of self worth as a member of the college community.

There are two important take-aways from Dominique's story. First, college can be about so much more than earning a degree. The relationships you build can have a dramatic impact on what you get out of your college career, both personally and professionally. Dominique's professors may one day be her colleagues, and her peers will soon be her professional network. Second, when you select a college, you are marrying into a second family. The college family you choose doesn't need to be perfect, but they do need to be there for you when you need them.

BREAK IT DOWN

Dominique

- *How is Dominique's experience with racism on campus different from Aubrey's?*
- *What did Dominique's school do differently that allowed her to feel welcomed and cared for on campus, compared to Aubrey's school?*
- *How has Dominique's school community supported her over the last four years?*

CHAPTER 11

Working Hard or Hardly Working

Out of the hundreds of students I have counseled, only one student blatantly stated that he didn't plan on working hard in college, and instead (in his own words), planned on going "buck wild." Suffice it to say, his comment elicited quite a few good-natured jokes regarding his anticipated social life. With the exception of "Buckie," I have never met a student who didn't honestly believe they were going to put forth their full effort in college. While working hard is important, the problem with saying you are going to work hard is that it is an unfocused statement. What are you going to work hard at? What does working hard look like? How do you measure working hard? Is it studying a certain number of hours per week? Is it being proactive in getting your homework done? Are those the same kind of choices you are making right now in high school? If not, what are you going to do to hold yourself accountable to your goals? In this chapter you will hear from two students in very different circumstances; both were confronted with challenges and had to find out if they had what it would take to meet their goals. While you are reading, ask yourself how these students' experiences differ from one another. Did these students have equal access to opportunity? What does it mean to work hard for each of them? If they gave up, what would the consequences be? How would it impact their future opportunities?

ISABEL

No Room for Failure

Lakemont College was actually like my last, last, last, last college choice. I literally applied just to include one more. I wasn't thinking about really going there. My number one choice was Penn State. I kinda almost didn't apply to Penn State, but the next thing you know I was accepted, and so I was like, "Great, this is where I am going." But once I got their financial aid letter, it wasn't what I was expecting. I talked to my mom and we both decided that I couldn't go. We decided on Lakemont College because of the financial aid. From then on, I knew I was going to Lakemont.

I had never even visited any of the colleges I applied to, which was a big mistake. That is something I regret, because this school's science department—I'm not trying to bash them—but Lakemont's science department is horrible. I mean, the scholarships they gave were so small, like $400, and they were so hard to get. I didn't think about how the school was religious, and being in the science department, those things just don't correlate together well. So, I do regret not visiting. I mean, I went on a senior field trip, but I didn't do a lot of research into the school.

Our lab equipment is horrible. I wouldn't say we are advanced at all. Even as a senior, my professor is bringing in stuff from another university, where she went to school. And that is not a good sign. We have professors that quit without notice. There is just a problem in the science department, not only with the faculty but with the department itself. I mean, we are always trying to get things like new equipment or lounges or things for the students, and it is a struggle with the school.

After I decided to go here, I talked a little bit with my high school chemistry teacher. She told me to think about going to Lakemont for two years and transferring to a school that I did want to go to. I was like, "OK, that honestly sounds like a good plan." So right off the bat I took the hardest classes: chem, bio, all that. Once the second year came, I would say I got comfortable with the school. I was like, "I'm already here. What's the point? Why spend more money? The money here is good; I shouldn't complain." So, that's what stopped me from transferring. I kept asking people, like my academic advisor, and they would ask me why I wanted to take out more loans at another school. They told me it's not where you graduate from, but what you do: your experience, your volunteering, etc. So then I was like, "OK, I won't go to Penn State."

They tell you that you can do volunteering or internships, but they don't give you the leads. It was mostly a do-it-yourself kinda thing. Part of it was that I didn't know what I was doing. I started to wonder what's the point. But then this last year, I got tired of telling myself what's the point. I told myself nobody is going to help me; I have to do it myself. I started researching internships myself. And this year I got three internships on my own. The first one was in a hospital in a microbiology lab; the second one was a summer internship that was paid; and the third one was with the Illinois State Police.

I would have loved to go to Penn State, and sometimes I still think, "Oh great, I am graduating from such a lower-ranking school." But I don't want to make myself feel that way. I'm president of the Red Cross at school here. I do love the fact that this is a small school. I know I learn better in a smaller school. I'm not going to become bitter: I'm going to make the best of it. I can't live thinking I spent four years at a college that I didn't want to go to. I don't want to live that way. I've met great people, and I've done great things that I'm not sure I would have done if I had gone to a different school. Once I got here, I was just thinking to myself, "I better make the best of it."

It's sad because a lot of my friends dropped out of school and chose jobs over school. But I kept looking at the bigger picture: the future. I kept asking, "What can I do to make my future better?" Because whatever you do today will impact tomorrow. So, I think because… I mean, I come from a background where

I will be the first to graduate from college, and seeing my family struggle painted a picture in my head. I knew I didn't want to be that. I may not know what I want to do, but I know I will graduate, own a house, and be able to travel. I just kept thinking about all these things I wanted in the future, and I didn't want to struggle working in fast food or in retail forever. I came up with this phrase: I love the struggle more than I hate the struggle, because you get so much out of the result. You might hate what you are going through, but you are going to love the result.

I never really got a lot of support from my mom, and my dad was addicted to drugs. It was always me and my sister. We raised ourselves. My mom said she would help me out with college, but the next thing you know, she's like, "I can't help you." So I found one job, and then another job. She never helped me. The only thing she paid for was the $100 deposit. After that, it was all me. Once she asked me for money, and I was upset, because she didn't know what I was going through. And I asked her, "Mom, do you even know how many jobs I have?" She was like, "I don't know, one or two." And I was like, "No, I have four jobs." How does my own mother not know how many jobs I have? It goes back to the family thinking going to school is easy. They would always ask me for favors: to do this or buy this. And from my perspective, I am working for something that they've never done; I'm working to better myself, to do better, and I don't think they see that.

That's how you can determine who you really are. I wasn't going to let bad things determine my behavior. Basically, what I am trying to say is you cause your own pain. If you don't want to suffer, don't suffer. It's that simple. But it is hard to put it into action. It's hard to apply it, but you have to apply the things you tell yourself. I am going to try as hard as I can so I won't have any regrets. I know it is going to be rough, but I don't want to think I could have tried harder. I can't look to my environment and think that there is something wrong with me. It all starts with me. If I want something better, I have to start with myself; I have to keep thinking positive.

Making The Most Of It

Moving on from a school that you were set on attending has to be one of the most difficult experiences in the college selection process. Getting denied by a college hurts, but for most of us we will smart a little bit, lick our wounds, and then move on. For some though, getting denied can be particularly devastating. Perhaps you were really stuck on a particular school and can't possibly envision yourself attending another college. Perhaps getting rejected was a little bit of an ego bruiser, especially if someone you knew was admitted and you weren't. Whatever the reason, having to move on from a school that you were stuck on can have lasting repercussions.

Unfortunately, I have watched students overlook really good opportunities because they were certain they would get admitted to a particular college. Many times these students fell short of the school's admission criteria, but had convinced themselves they were going to be admitted based on an unrealistic conversations with admissions reps or positive campus visit experiences. These students mistook politeness for encouragement and ended up putting all their eggs in one basket. I've seen students completely stop applying to college, skip scholarship essays, opt-out of campus visit opportunities, all because they were sure they had found "the one."

The only thing worse than getting denied is having to turn down admission from your dream school. This is what Isabel had to do. The pain and disappointment runs deep. Isabel had to turn away from a particular path that she so desperately wanted to follow. She did everything right. She was accepted to her dream school, and she just couldn't afford it. When a student has to turn down their dream school, it almost always boils down to one thing: money. Isabel didn't throw in the towel immediately. I have to tell you, we spent a lot of time trying to find some way to make the math work. It just couldn't add up. The gap in funding was just too big. Eventually, it became clear that there was nothing more to be done. It's important to realize when to keep fighting, and when to move on and trust that the universe has something more spectacular planned for you.

Isabel's story is perhaps the one that remains closest to me heart. It's a simple story with an ambiguous ending. But, it is also a tale of peace—the peace that can be found when one lets go of an unrequited future and focuses on the joy in every small step forward.

BREAK IT DOWN

Isabel

- *What do you think is the moral of Isabel's story?*
- *What aspects of Isabel's story resonate with you most?*
- *What do you think keeps Isabel so positive?*
- *Do you think Isabel will finish her last semester and graduate?*
- *Do you think Isabel would have had a different college experience if she had been able to go away to college?*
- *Why or why not?*

ERIC

Hard Today, Harder Tomorrow

I had never heard of Fenston University before. Not ever. So I applied, and I ended up being accepted, and it was like this big thing. It kinda star struck me a little bit. And I thought, "OK, this is actually a big deal, especially with the full ride and everything." I had never even visited before I was accepted. I'd been accepted to Fenston and some small schools, but once I looked into it, I was like, "Wow Fenston is actually a really good school."

Honestly, I like Fenston because it is eye opening to how the world really works. People at Fenston are very competitive. You have to be the best at what you want to do. You have to be better than everyone else. It is a very competitive environment. It's very business focused. Not only are you supposed to know what you are doing now, but you are supposed to know what you are going to do in the next few years. People already had grad school classes that they were planning on taking, and they were just freshmen. I was like, "What am I going to wear the first day of class?" Everyone else was just so future-focused. That was definitely eye opening. That helped me realize what I had to focus on and what I needed to do.

In the first couple days in our dorms, they brought everybody together and were like, "What did you do over the summer?" Then everyone was like, "I went skydiving, I went scuba-diving," and all these amazing things. Then when it came to me, I was like, "Oh I hung out with my family." I just felt out of place. To hear everyone's amazing stories and then for me to do something so not amazing—yeah. Campus was a little intimidating. When you go to public universities there is a larger group of people that look like you. The main thing, at Fenston, there is just a lot of White people. My first few days I didn't see any other Latino students.

I was in the dorms and I was hoping that I would get a roommate, and they would force me to get to know people, but they ended up giving me a room by myself. It was like my little fortress I could go to and be alone. My first quarter was good, but I didn't make any connections, and that is something I regret, for sure. My friend brought me to the multi-cultural center, which is where all the minorities go to hang out and meet each other. That's where I ended up meeting so many cool people. I started building up my friend group. One of the guys I saw as an older brother told me about this fraternity. It took two years, but I finally joined. I feel like that was a milestone for my college career. Once I joined I definitely became much more social, a lot more outgoing.

I ended up joining the fraternity, but there were a couple bumps after that. It takes a lot of your time. I was more into the fraternity than trying to get my school work done, so I was already on academic warning. I ended up not getting my grades up enough, and got kicked out. I was on warning one quarter, and then they told me I had to get my grades up or have consequences; mine was getting kicked out. It was horrible. It totally shook my world. I had no idea what to do. After that I had one goal in mind, and that was to get readmitted.

So, I went to a community college. It was a horrible commute. It was like 45 minutes to an hour on the bus. It was a tough time. I still had to work to pay my lease. So I had to work and still go to school. It was over the summer, and I was working at a moving company. It was very physically taxing. Luckily the classes at the community college weren't difficult. I took a math class and a science class. I took those two classes and was working, just trying to get back into school. I ended up doing really well in the classes: I got two As. I went back to the board and asked for an appeal. I had to write a whole statement explaining why my grades had gone down and all that. I explained that I couldn't take more classes at the community college because I had to work to pay for everything. I met with the board and they ended up accepting me back.

It seemed like the fairytale happy ending, but it definitely wasn't. I was more focused on... I was just so happy to be back, instead of being like, "Okay you've got to make a change." it was more like a celebration for me the whole time. I ended up partying all the time and not really doing what I was supposed to be doing. And so the quarter after I got back in, I ended up getting kicked out again. Yeah, I know. I didn't make any changes. I mean, I did study more, but it definitely wasn't enough.

I don't know how it happened; I mean, I do know how it happened. I ended up smoking a lot of weed. It wasn't just casually smoking; it was like everyday, for a good amount of the day. There were days when I would wake up and just be like, "I don't feel like going to class today." I honestly don't know what was going on. It felt like I was just on pause while everything passed me by. It was pretty bad. I knew it was bad, but I just kept going back to it. I just kept smoking. One of the people I met was a big smoker, but he definitely had his stuff together. He got me into smoking. Then I got into it a little too much, and I wasn't focused on studying.

So then I got kicked out again. And I was like, "Dam, how could this happen again? I just went through this!" There was a lot of talking to myself and trying to figure out what to do. After that, once again my one goal was to get back in. I got kicked out in the winter, so in the spring I went to the board and tried to get back in, and they said, "No, you can't just get back in again this time. You are going to have to prove that you can be successful." So, spring quarter I just worked, because I was still on my lease. During the summer, I took a math course on campus, but I didn't pay for it. I told the professor my situation, and I asked if I could just audit it because I couldn't really afford it. He said, "Yes." I ended up getting a B in the class. I went back to community college in the fall, took three classes, and did well in those. I went back to Fenston to appeal, and they said no again. And then they said, "You can only appeal one more time, so you need to wait a whole year or two before you try again."

There was one thing that was really eye opening. I actually ended up going to jail for three days. It was related to drugs. Having your schedule set out for you, not having the freedom to do what you want when you want to—that was the pivotal point. To see the bars, to only be able to eat at a certain time, and if you don't eat you are not eating for the rest of the day, not being able to move outside of this little square—it was a horrible experience. I would say that my lowest point was my first night in jail. I just laid in my bed, and there were so many scenarios that went through my head about how I had messed up my life. I honestly thought I had no chance to fix it. It was definitely a changing point. I had a lot of time to think, and so I ended up reading this self-help book—one of those cheesy self-empowering books from the little library there. I ended up reading through half of it, and I began thinking, "Maybe this is not too bad." This one story was about this guy who got busted for drugs and then ended up starting this company that made millions. And I was thinking maybe I'm not going to do that exact same thing, but if he could do it, I definitely can do it. Once I got out, I was like, "I need to get my stuff together."

I ended up taking two economics courses at the community college. I also enrolled in this online math course. You take a test that shows what you are good at and what you need to work on, and it designs a little course for you. I went back to the board of appeals, and I showed them all my receipts and everything I did. At the end of winter they ended up readmitting me.

The first time I was kicked out I just did everything they told me to do to get back in. The second time it was like, obviously there is something you need to change in yourself. Get yourself in order. The second time was much more of a focus on changing myself. Now, I am actually trying to start a company with one of my friends who already graduated. Right now I am only focusing on school and the business. I am on court supervision, so I can't get into trouble for the next two years. After that, my record will be expunged. Now that I am back, a big motivator for me is my family. If I can actually make money *in the future, I can take care of my family. That's a pretty big motivator for me.*

It feels so great to be back. Honestly, I am so excited for this year to start. I have a lot of goals right now that I want to reach.

The Only Way To Go Is Up

There are a few big lessons we can learn from Eric. First, there is a fine line between liberating behavior and self-destructive behavior. If you don't know where that is, dial it back until you can figure it out. So you may miss a few parties; it sure beats sitting in jail. Second, don't waste second chances. They don't come cheaply. In Eric's case, it will cost him over a year of his life, and a lot of money. Third, it's really hard to rebuild your image after you've messed up.

Before you judge Eric, there is something you should know. I would never have guessed that Eric would have made the kind of mistakes he made. Eric was a kind of guy with just the right amount of teenage awkwardness to be endearing and annoying at the same time. He was incredibly bright without being a know-it-all. He was the kind of kid that seemed to have it together without being driven to the point of anxiety attacks. He might have earned a few eye-rolls from me over the years, but I never once worried about whether he would be successful in college.

Let's be real. Eric smoked too much weed, got arrested, and got kicked out of an awesome school. It's definitely not what I would have expected (and I am sure he would say the same thing), but he didn't kill anyone. On the range of bad decisions, it's probably a 6 out of 10: bad enough to carry serious repercussions, but not bad enough for his mother to disown him. I am being picky here, because I think it is important to understand that everyday, "normal" kids do stupid stuff, and they do it for reasons they aren't even really aware of. The frightening reality is Eric had a lot of opportunity on the table, and when he made his mistakes he almost lost it all.

So, what could Eric have done? Undoubtedly, he could have made different choices about his recreational activities. But there is another issue here that is more important. Eric needed help, and he never got it. At some point it became obvious that he needed help getting back on track. Eric's struggles are exactly why student counseling services are available. Whether Eric could have used a peer group on balancing social life and academics, or whether he needed one-on-one mental-health or substance abuse counseling, student counseling-services would have been a valuable resource.

Many students I have worked with have expressed resistance to the idea of seeking out help from the campus counseling center. When I pry a little bit into why, I find their hesitation is often rooted in concern for what their family and friends might think. These are not empty concerns. If you come from a family where mental health counseling is taboo, it can be very difficult to overcome that. However, you should know that student health services and counseling services are confidential. These services are already paid for as a part of your school fees. Therefore, even if you are still on your parent's insurance, student counseling services should not need to bill your insurance, and absolutely will not contact your parents unless you ask them to.

When I was an undergrad I really struggled with depression. It was debilitating. Reaching out to student counseling services was an incredibly difficult decision. I kept hearing my mother's disapproval and anger in my mind. But at some point I realized that I needed to be healthy—and finish my degree—and that was more important than someone else's approval. And so I started seeing a counselor, and it completely changed my life. In fact, it probably saved my life. If you have been raised to put others first, or their opinions first, it might be very difficult to put yourself first. But, your health (and yes mental health is health) outweighs anyone else's opinion.

As for rebuilding his image, Eric is still in the early stages of doing what he needs to get things back on track. The good news is Eric has been re-admitted to school, and he has some time before he hits the job market. Eric is still on probation and will be for a few more years. Keeping a clean record and getting his arrest expunged are vital steps for Eric's employment prospects.

Unfortunately, Eric can't stop there. We live in the age of social media, where a year sowing your oats can be very difficult to scrub from the Internet. You, as a prospective college student, might be in the same boat. Youth is about spreading your wings and making decisions on your own, and some of those decisions might be mistakes. However, your mistakes are the perfect fuel to feed the world's unquenchable thirst for schadenfreude (pleasure in someone else's pain). It sucks. It's not fair, and if you had been born before 1980, things would have been very different. But you weren't born before 1980, and for that I'm sorry. We got anonymity; you get iPhones. That's just how it is.

BREAK IT DOWN
Eric

- *What do you think are the big lessons to learn from Eric's experience?*
- *What advice would you have given Eric if he were your friend or roommate?*
- *Why didn't Eric get back on track when he was re-admitted the first time?*
- *What is Eric doing differently now?*
- *Do you think he will stay on track and graduate? Why or why not?*

Chapter 12

Belonging

The world can be a very difficult place when you don't feel like you belong. If you are brave enough to be true to yourself and your story, you may not always be accepted by those around you. Being rejected by your peers can be devastating, but fear of rejection can be particularly damaging. When we feel like we don't belong, our normal response it to withdraw and protect ourselves from potentially hurtful interactions. But the more we withdraw to protect ourselves, the more isolated we become from people and resources that can help us. The emotional turmoil and fear of not belonging can be especially devastating in college, where most students already feel disconnected from their family, friends, and the social supports they previously relied on to maintain a healthy sense of self.

In this chapter we will hear from two students who had to navigate being singled out from their peers. As you are reading, reflect on a time when you felt out of place or different from your peers.

- How did you feel?

- How did you respond?

- What would you do if you found yourself in a similar situation?

EMMY

Culture Shock

Starting off, Lavigne was not my first choice. It wasn't even like my tenth choice. Lavigne was a safety college for me. A lot of stuff ended up happening last minute, and I ended up not going to my first choice school. Already I was pretty pessimistic about going to Lavigne. I am gay, and obviously you can tell that I'm gay. So, I got to Lavigne and I liked it from the start. It's a liberal arts school, but for being a liberal arts school, people here aren't really open-minded at all. It was hard adjusting and meeting new friends. I am a very 'out there' person, and I was always in sports and clubs. Coming to Lavigne was hard because there were already cliques. And people assumed—well, I looked gay, so obviously I was gay—and they assumed I would hang out with "the gay group." Yeah. Those are like the theater kids, and I completely did not do that at all. I did my own thing. And people would get mad at me that I wouldn't go to LGBT meetings or any of that. So that was kinda funny.

I actually still don't have a group. I really get along with my suite mates though. I did join softball this term, so I'm becoming friends with them. Our classes are really small here at Lavigne. Sometimes, honestly, I am scared to raise my hand in class, because I don't want the professor to say, "You look like a he" or use "he" pronouns; it's kinda embarrassing. Like, sometimes that would happen. But, my roommate is on the soccer team—and she is really popular—so a lot of people have gotten to know me now, and so they don't identify me as "he" anymore. At Lavigne we do this weird thing: during the first week of school we say our names and we say our pronouns. Of course, I may look like a different gender, but I still definitely know I am a girl, and prefer "she" and "her." Definitely when I say that out loud I do get looks, and it's kind of uncomfortable. I used to get mad. Like, everyone would look straight in the classroom, and I would be the only one who would look gay, and then they would say, "Oh yeah, don't forget to say your pronouns." And I would be like, "Are you just saying that because I am in the classroom?"

It was not like that in high school at all. In high school I was president of groups and played sports. My high school was small, and that made it easier. Here, my professors don't know who I am. I'm just a freshman, and so they don't know what I am capable of. It's a lot of getting used to, having to put your reputation out there. Freshman and sophomore year of high school is when I came out and completely changed my look. Freshman year I was number one in the class, so all the teachers knew I was smart and knew who I was. Sophomore year, it was the same thing. So when I changed my look, nothing else really changed. My classmates didn't really change. Guys thought my look was cool. Girls thought I was cooler. I'm just a really goofy person, and I like to make people laugh. I don't go with just one group of people; I like to go with everyone. People like me when they get to know me. But when they don't know me, they can feel intimidated.

I have a very strong personality. A lot of the friends I have become really close to here have told me that I intimidate people, and so people don't speak to me. In the classroom I am speaking up a lot more, but here…its not just being gay; it's also being Hispanic. I take a lot of computer science classes, and in my computer science classes I am the only Hispanic. There are no African American or Hispanic students. It's all White and Asian, and so it's even a lot more uncomfortable. It's also hard being a female in my computer science classes. There were a lot of international students who would say out loud that they thought women shouldn't be taking classes. So it was hard: one, being female; two, being gay; and three, being Hispanic. Usually the professor would just ignore the students' comments. I used to get mad, but I mean, it's their traditions. It's where they're from. I have definitely had to learn to be more patient.

In high school I had a lot more guy friends. I have no idea why. Okay, I'm going to be honest: a lot of girls here check me out. I mean, I think they are just curious, like, "Oh, a new toy." Most of them are upperclassmen. A lot of gay people here are not out. They just stick to themselves. But, I'm more out there. So, I have a lot of girls around me. It makes me feel awkward, because I know what they want. I've always been super cool with guys, so I'm not sure. The guys just seem to shy away.

Most of the people here are not from the city, so it's their first time seeing a butch girl or whatever, and then it's also their first time seeing a Hispanic or whatever. I have friends who have never seen more than a few Hispanics in their life. When I tell them that my parents are pastors, then it's a whole other thing, and I have to explain to them that I can be gay as well as religious. It's pretty funny. We have a lot of international students here; so, we definitely have a lot of people who are Muslim or Jewish, or whatever. But, we also have people who are from small towns and just don't understand different ways other than their own. You also have people who are gay, but still closed-minded. I met this guy when I was working at the cafeteria this weekend who broke up with his boyfriend because he thought he was sinning. He didn't think he should be around other gay people. It's unbelievable.

I want to become a diplomat. If not, then I plan to go to law school. It caught me off guard, since I came from a high school where people knew me because of rugby and soccer. I was outspoken, and everyone knew my views. I thought that coming to college I was going to fit in. So it threw me off. I thought I was really good at knowing people and different cultures, but it was like, "Nope. No you're not; sit down." So, I guess it's good. It has changed my views.

To Thine Own Self Be True

Emmy is outgoing, charismatic, intelligent, mature, and wonderfully funny. She is also gay, the daughter of pastors, Hispanic, and pursuing a career in a male-dominated field. Emmy likes her college, but has had a difficult time adjusting socially. From the outside, it's kind of difficult to see any evidence that Emmy is struggling at all. She is incredibly close to her suite mates, who are very popular on campus, and have introduced her to a wide circle of acquaintances. She has joined the softball team, and is considering joining the soccer team in the spring. She is constantly surrounded by young women who are smitten with her. It's hard to imagine how Emmy could be doing much better. And yet, Emmy is struggling.

It seems to me that Emmy's struggles are more about feeling out of place than feeling lonely. Emmy landed in a college where the social rules were driven by gender stereotypes. In high school Emmy had friends of both genders, but tended to hang with the guys more often. In college the guys seem to shy away from her; instead Emmy's social circle is full of "straight" young ladies, some of whom behave in a non-platonic way towards Emmy. In high school no one questioned Emmy's appearance. The fact that Emmy identifies as a female, but has a more masculine aesthetic, was a non-issue. In college, Emmy's appearance seems to be the only thing that people notice. College has introduced Emmy to an entirely new world of gender-based socializing that she isn't sure she is comfortable with. It's like Emmy showed up to a party ready to line dance, only to find that everyone else was waltzing. #awkward.

Being the only butch female in her college was just the first social norm that Emmy had to navigate. Emmy is also Hispanic in a majority White college campus. She is also one of the only females in a male-dominated department. When Emmy headed off to a liberal arts college, she was expecting a liberal-minded college. What she encountered was quite the opposite. But this is exactly what a liberal arts school is designed to be: a place where individuals from all different walks of life can meet at the crossroads of diversity and learn from each other. Emmy is exposed to new cultures, backgrounds, perspectives, and social norms that she never would have been exposed to at a more urban school. And however awkward Emmy may feel amongst her new peers, they seem to have really welcomed her into their social circles. Lastly, Emmy's small classes have forced her to engage with people that she may have otherwise avoided at a larger university. These experiences, while uncomfortable, are important situations for Emmy to navigate—especially if she plans to become a diplomat.

In our conversation, Emmy emphasized the importance of going to see your college campus before making a decision. Emmy attributes her ability to be successful at Lavigne to her strong sense of self and self-confidence. Emmy didn't change to make anyone else feel comfortable, and she didn't hide who she was either. She approached college with an open mind and heart. But Emmy is also quick to say that a small college may not be for everyone, especially if a student is struggling with issues of identity. In Emmy's experience, small colleges are places where everyone knows everyone, and that might not offer the level of anonymity that some students seek.

BREAK IT DOWN

Emmy

- Why is Emmy uncomfortable around her school peers?
- How can Emmy address this discomfort?
- What kind of stereotypes do you think Emmy encounters as a gay, Hispanic, engineering major?
- How would you navigate these stereotypes if you were in her shoes?

SOPHIA

All I Have Ever Wanted

I remember I really wanted to go to high school. My siblings—they didn't really get to take advantage of their education. They were in another country, and they wanted to help my mom pay for bills. And so, I was the first daughter to go to high school. That was really huge for me. I remember I didn't know a lot about college. I didn't really have anyone who was there to guide me or to help me. So, high school was big for me. One thing that stuck out to me when I started high school, on the first day, the principal got us in the multipurpose room, and I remember the first day of orientation they made us go onto the stage and say to our advisory, "I will graduate with you in four years." I remember Celia was with me, and when we graduated with each other, it was so emotional, because we remembered that day. I remember how they told us, "You are going to graduate high school, but you are also going to graduate from college." They really prepared me for that—for example, how they doubled up on math, doubled up on reading, the resources of staying after school if you didn't do your homework. Looking back on it, it's so worth it.

I remember we had to apply to seven different universities, but being undocumented I didn't have the money, and my parents weren't really supportive. It was devastating. I attended this high school that was like, from the first day, you are going to graduate and you are going to go to college. I felt like I had worked so hard for nothing. And then, just seeing all my friends get acceptance letters, I was happy for them, but I felt like…my parents are hard workers, and I wanted to make them proud. I wanted to say, "Mom, you worked so hard for me; I'm going to buy you your house." I wanted to say that, and I couldn't.

Being undocumented, I didn't have a job, and I didn't have the nine digits. So, I was stuck. This was before DACA. There was nothing. It was just, learning how to think outside of the box. I remember having arguments with my parents and telling them I wanted to go to Illinois Park University. I remember when I got the letter for the admissions interview. I didn't know if I could go to the interview, because I didn't know how to get there. Then we looked at how transportation worked, and we sat down and looked up the train schedule. My mom and I went to the interview, and we connected with people when we were there. My advisor was really awesome, and I told her my story, and she actually worked at the flea market where we used to work. She was like, "Just talk to this lady at the Latino Resource center and she will get you connected." I didn't want to call her, but I did. She said, "I have this other student who was in your same situation, and she's now a sophomore, and she's actually looking for a roommate." I remember crying and thanking God, and being like, "God, this is all I ever wanted—an education."

But, things did get harder. I didn't have all the friends that other students had. I commuted, which was a way out of paying for the dorms and the meal plan and all of that. But my roommate was a sophomore, and she already had friends. The friends I met would ask "Where's your dorm?" or questions that normal freshmen ask, and I felt like I needed to lie. I felt like I couldn't connect with them in that area. I would tell them that my dad would pick me up, and that was why I couldn't hang out after class. That was really hard. Also, there were little things with being undocumented. I remember when I went to get my school ID, they wouldn't give me one with a picture on it. That was really devastating. When I would ride the campus shuttle, they would ask me to show my ID, and my ID didn't have a picture, so they would say, "Your ID isn't valid." My friends would all show each other their IDs, and then they would want to know why my ID didn't have a picture. It pointed me out from everyone else; it made me different. And I didn't want to tell everyone my story; I didn't know them. I felt like I had to tell everyone I met that I was undocumented, or I would have to lie. Every department of the university, it was the same. I felt like, "Why are they treating me differently?" That was hard. I didn't want it to define me, so I would just bottle it up. Later, that became a problem. Like when my mom got sick, and broke her wrist. We didn't have insurance for her surgery, so we had to pay for it. My dad would work double, but it wasn't enough, and I remember I had to apply for a lot of scholarships. The hardest part about the scholarships was telling my story—being vulnerable in like 300 words, or 500 words. I would feel like, "How am I supposed to tell you my whole life in 300 words? I am more than that."

When I first got to Illinois Park my grades actually went up. I was like "Yes, I got this; this is what I want to do." Then, I would not know if I was going to have the money to be back the next semester; it was hard. When my mom got sick, there were things that would happen that didn't allow me to perform at my best. I would come back each semester and my grades would go up, and then something else would happen, and they would go back down. When I left Illinois Park it was heartbreaking, but at the same time it was a relief because I knew I was going to take care of myself first, and in order to perform at my best, I needed to take care of myself.

I noticed that I wasn't going to Bible study anymore. God plays a big role in my life, and I was a Bible study leader, and I had to step down from that. I wouldn't want to hang out with friends. I wanted to be alone. The topic of immigration, I avoided it. I didn't want to know anything about it. I just started feeling really lonely. If I had a really bad exam, I would be really hard on myself. And I would be like, "I'm just going to be like everyone else. I'm going to be a failure." I just kept thinking, "I'm going to have to work at a factory my whole life." I don't know. There would be moments when I would tell a professor that I wasn't doing well, or I wasn't feeling well, and they would just treat me like I was making an excuse. I would just break down. I would go sit by the pond and cry. I would tell God, "This hurts so much; why do you keep wanting me to talk about this? You already know my story; you already know what I have been through. Why is it necessary for me to keep talking about it?" But that's when I realized that it was the healing process. Deep down, those lies and those stereotypes, were buried, and I felt like He just wanted me to let go. I would wake up in the morning and be like, "Today is going to be a better day;" but then I would have so much anxiety about going to class and be afraid I was going to cry in class. That's when I realized I needed help. If I wanted to move on, I needed to let my parents love me and my friends love me. That was the hardest part of all.

I don't think my friends could have done anything more, because they were there for me. But, I could have done more. I could have been open with them and talked. I got to a point where I was tired of fighting. I had to fight all through high school, and in college, and then thinking ahead about med school; I was just tired of fighting. I didn't want to fight anymore. Before I left, I remember telling my parents that I was depressed, and it wasn't just a type of sadness. And they didn't understand. They didn't know what depression was. Then a friend passed away, and that was my breaking point. I wanted to go home; I wanted to take care of myself. I thought when I got home that I would feel better, but I just felt worse. I felt much worse. I remember it was a Sunday, and I broke down crying, and I kept telling my Mom, "I don't feel well." And then she broke down crying with me. And that was so hard for her to cry in front of me. We realized we were broken and that we needed each other.

There were days when my family just wouldn't understand, when my mom would just be like, "Why are you crying? I don't understand; you were fine before." There were days when I would just cry, but I didn't know how to explain what was going on. Then I decided to go to therapy. That was the first step. I knew I was at a place, and I didn't know how to get out of it. I told the therapist my situation, why I left Illinois Park and everything. What was cool about seeing her was that I was able to talk about God, because she was a therapist who was also spiritual. That really helped me. I remember just telling myself,

"OK, now I want to go back to school." I was feeling better, and I was ready to go back.

I had the choice of returning to Illinois Park or staying here and going to a community college. It was a hard decision. I had started volunteering at the children's hospital here, and I knew I wouldn't be able to do that back at Illinois Park. The hospital was helping me so much: to see myself in the future. I really wanted to keep working at the hospital. Also, just thinking about how I was going to have to keep a job—it is harder to find work at Illinois Park. I don't know. Just thinking about those things I sorta just went with my gut and chose to stay here. Now I have DACA, so I can work at the museum. My coworkers there are so supportive, and they just keep pushing me when I have to go from work to school. They are like, "You've got this; you're going to ace that exam." If I didn't have DACA I wouldn't have been able to work at all. I have to pay out of pocket for school, but I'm used to it.

I'm still going to go to med school. Being a physician is God's calling for me. I know it. I used to doubt it. I'd be like, "God, why do you want me to be a physician when I am undocumented, and people see me as the lowest and not wanted?" Deep down inside I always wanted to be a physician, but I doubted myself. And then at Illinois Park God showed me. Every time I would be like, "How am I going to pay for school?" a phone would ring, and there would be a scholarship. I felt like I was just being thrown fireballs, and I had to go for it.

Winning a Rigged Game

By now you are probably really good at identifying choices students could have made to handle challenging situations. You might think that Sophia should never have gone away to college. You might think that she should have gone to the school administration to complain about the discrimination she was experiencing. You might think that Sophia should never have left school, and instead should have sought out counseling on campus. You might be thinking a lot of things, and I applaud you for putting your problem-solving hat on. But I want to take a moment and reveal a truth lurking in the shadows of this story: Sophia didn't do anything wrong. It wasn't wrong for her to dream about going to college. It wasn't wrong for her to dream about med school. It wasn't wrong for her to want to be treated like every other student on campus. It wasn't wrong for her to hold out hope that things would get better. And it wasn't wrong for her to come home when she realized they weren't.

Not all undocumented students will have the exact same experience as Sophia. Some colleges are more inclusive and supportive of their students. Not all undocumented students will face the same family stressors as Sophia. This story is not included to illustrate Sophia's mistakes. Instead, Sophia's story is included to illustrate the very real effects of public policy on your ability to succeed as a student, from student loan interest rates to who qualifies for federal student aid. Sometimes decisions are simply out of your hands, and sometimes those decisions impact your ability to succeed as a student.

After reading this book, I hope you feel very well prepared to choose a good quality school and handle the personal and academic issues that might arise while you are in college. However, you won't be truly prepared to take on unforeseen challenges unless you know what to do when the game is rigged. Sophia didn't fail; Sophia figured out a way to win in a game that was set up for her to fail. If DACA had been policy when Sophia had left for college, she would have been able to work and participate in department-mandated internships. Two years after Sophia went off to college the state began issuing undocumented residents with state issued IDs. If such a policy had been in place when Sophia went off to college, she would have been allowed a school ID with a photo, thus granting her access to the campus shuttle, the library, the dorms, and other campus buildings from which she was excluded. If both of these policies had happened just a few years earlier, Sophia's story may have ended very differently.

But, these policies were not in place for Sophia. At some point she realized the game had not been set up in a way to help her succeed; it had been set up to keep her from succeeding. Instead of giving up, she changed tactics. She looked at her surroundings and positioned herself in the place that would grant her the most access to the academic, emotional, and financial resources she needed to meet her goals, and earn her degree.

BREAK IT DOWN

Sophia

- *How is Sophia's story similar to Dominique's and Aubrey's story? How is it different?*
- *Do you think Sophia did the right thing by coming home?*
- *How did school policies affect Sophia's experiences in college?*
- *How did state policy affect Sophia's experiences in college?*
- *How did national policy affect Sophia's experiences in college?*
- *What kind of policies will affect you in college (think school-level, state, and national)?*
- *If you were to propose one policy to increase college graduation rates for students like yourself, what would it be?*

The Art of Graduating

If graduating from college was easy, everyone would do it, and we wouldn't have colleges where 90% of students don't graduate. Struggling in college is normal. Getting through the struggle is imperative. In the last few chapters you have heard from a number of smart and capable students who have all struggled in college. Their stories are included in this book precisely because they are not unique. They are the same kind of stories I have heard again and again. Students like Eric, struggle because of their own poor choices. You can only hope they get themselves back on track before the consequences have life-long consequences. Students like Dominique are struggling to handle severe family trauma while fighting to stay motivated and invested in their education. Students like Isabel are struggling to make the most of a less than ideal situation in a less than ideal world. And other students, like Aubrey and Sophia, are simultaneously struggling against the injustices of the external world, and the emotional devastation of their internal world.

No matter what your struggle, you should never feel the burden of having to get through it alone. Counseling resources, mentorship, social groups, and religious groups can all play a vital role in supporting you emotionally. If one resource doesn't feel right seek out another, and another, and another until you get what you need. Reach back to old teachers, religious leaders, or community organizations where you used to be a member. Connect to those people who can lift your confidence and remind you of how valuable you are and how capable you can be. And most of all, love yourself. Be your own advocate. Speak up. Call people out when they are not treating you well. Choose happiness. Fun is situational; happiness is a state of being. Stand up for yourself and your ability to do well in school. Stand up to those individuals in your life that threaten your ability to do well in school (even if that someone is you). Be honest with yourself about your abilities, your needs, and your limitations. Forget shame. Shame is nothing more than a weight in your pocket that you can choose to carry, or choose to toss aside.

SECTION 3

COLLEGE KNOWLEDGE

CHAPTER 13

Tips, Tricks, and Tools

This chapter is a collage of resources and tools aimed at helping you navigate the bumps in the college application process. Everything from keeping your applications in order, to crafting a good essay, to handling campus bureaucracy is woven together into a makeshift quilt of college knowledge.

The materials in this chapter are organized in this order:

- **Before You Apply**
- **Preparing to Apply**
    - The College Application Process
    - The College Application Timeline
    - Application Tips
- **Presenting Yourself as a Candidate**
    - Writing Your College Essays
    - Asking for a Letter of Recommendation
    - College Fair Card Template
    - Practice Pitches for College Fairs
    - Colleges that Offer Fly-Out Programs
- **Paying for College**
    - The Financial Aid Process
    - Financial Aid Checklist for Senior Year
    - Paying for College (Non-US Citizens)
    - Tuition Deposit Plan
- **Applying**
    - Password Sheet
    - College Application Tracker
- **Decision Time**
    - Interpreting Award Letters
    - Comparing Your Options
    - College Matriculation Checklist

Before You Apply

Before you even get started with applications, there are some steps that should be completed first. For instance, you are going to need an admissions essay and personal statement. Additionally, you will need to make plans for visiting with college representatives, either on the college campus or at a college fair. You need to know how to deal with colleges and their employees in a professional but productive way. As you make your way through the college application process you may find yourself getting the run-around. If so, it is important to know how to handle such a situation, or even better how to avoid it entirely. Lastly, now is the time to start thinking about saving for your tuition deposit. Most tuition deposits are a few hundred dollars. You need a plan for where you are going to get that money, and you need to make sure that plan is feasible.

Preparing to Apply

The College Application Process

Before you start hitting the "submit" button on a slew of college applications, let's quickly go over the steps to the application process:
1. **Determine the colleges you want to apply to.** If you read Chapter 3 then you probably already have a head start on your application list. Remember your application list is customized to you based on your GPA and test-scores.
2. **Write, edit, proof, and finalize your personal statement and admissions essay.** If you are feeling lost or overwhelmed with the idea of summing up your life in 500 words and wowing complete strangers at the same time, have no fear! There are some worksheets to help you with writing your essays included in this chapter.

3. **Determine if you will be using the Common App.** The Common App is a single application that you can submit to multiple schools. I strongly urge you to use the Common App whenever possible. To see if your schools accept the Common App go to commonapp.org and search for your schools.
4. **Secure letters of recommendations.** Most colleges require that you submit letters of recommendations from teachers, coaches, or other school officials who can vouch for your academic abilities and your character. Make sure you ask at least one academic teacher for a recommendation if possible. There is a sample recommendation request form that you can use later in this chapter.
5. **Complete your applications.** This sounds simple, but it is anything but simple. Colleges—even those that accept the Common App—often want additional essays or materials specific to their admissions process. Also, every school will have different deadlines for admissions. Early Action and Regular Admissions are the most common types of admissions and do not require you to attend a school just because you are admitted. Early Decision is different. If you apply Early Decision you are legally committing to that school if they accept you. You can only apply Early Decision to one college. Your other applications have to be either Early Action or Regular Admissions.

The College Application Timeline

Below is a general timeline for students applying for regular decision or early action (not early decision). These dates serve as a general template. In addition, you will need to research, know, and keep track of all your college deadlines to ensure you do not miss any important submission deadlines.

Once you submit an application, keep track of your submissions on the following pages.

SEPTEMBER (Junior Year)
- Begin studying for ACT/SAT

DECEMBER (Junior Year)
- If you have a 3.5 GPA or higher, go to the following websites and read the process for applying to:
  - Posse Foundation www.possefoundation.org
  - Gates Millennium Scholarship www.gmsp.org
  - Quest Bridge Scholarship www.questbridge.org

JUNE (Summer Before Senior Year)
- Complete personal essay exercises

JULY (Summer Before Senior Year)
- Complete rough draft of personal essay

AUGUST (Summer Before Senior Year)
- Rewrite draft of essay
- Search for NACAC fee waiver online. Read the eligibility and print several copies of the waiver if you are eligible. You will need to submit these with your application if you are not using the Common App.

SEPTEMBER (Senior Year)
- Identify your college application strategy
- Identify potential colleges using application strategy
- Research colleges
- Request letters of recommendation
- Submit essay to adult for editing/feedback

OCTOBER (Senior Year)
- Submit FAFSA / CSS profile
- Fill in college application checklist
- Identify colleges with early deadlines
- Complete at least one college application
- Submit NACAC fee waivers to counselor
- Complete final version of personal essay

NOVEMBER (Senior Year)
- Complete at least four more college applications
- Submit NACAC fee waivers to counselor
- Update college application tracker

DECEMBER (Senior Year)
- Complete remaining college applications
- Submit NACAC fee waivers to counselor
- Update college application tracker

JANUARY (Senior Year)
- Apply for scholarships (www.fastweb.com)
- Update college application tracker

FEBRUARY (Senior Year)
- Update college application tracker
- Update / link FAFSA
- Submit requested financial aid verification

MARCH-APRIL (Senior Year)
- Review award letters
- Ready funds for tuition deposit

By MAY 1ST (Senior Year)
- Accept admissions (see matriculation checklist)
- Pay tuition deposit

Application Tips

Application Fee Waiver

Colleges charge application fees to apply for admissions. These fees can add up and become cost prohibitive. If finances are tight, you may be able to obtain a fee waiver. Some schools will make you complete their own fee waiver, but most will accept a NACAC fee waiver submitted by your counselor. Download and print several copies of the waiver (just search for NACAC fee waiver). Complete the top portion and have your counselor complete the rest. Have your counselor include this fee waiver with your transcripts.

If ANY of the following applies to your family, you are eligible for a NACAC fee waiver:
- Receives free or reduced lunch
- Eligible for ACT/SAT fee waiver
- Eligible for SNAP (food stamps)
- Receives TANF (public assistance)
- Lives in subsidized housing
- Is in foster care
- Financial hardship

Applications

Pay close attention to those short answer questions on your applications. Short answer questions are often a way for colleges to catch a sneak-peak at your unedited writing style. Colleges know that many students get help editing their college essays, but often overlook getting feedback on the short-answer questions. Colleges are hoping that your short answer questions will give them an inside view into your unedited writing abilities.

The Common App is a fantastic way to save some time on applications, but the rewards come with high risks. Do it well, and you save a lot of time and headache. Do it poorly, and you diminish your chances for acceptance at all of your schools.

Bureaucracy 101

If you call to speak with an admissions or financial aid counselor, and they haven't asked you for your name, birthdate, or social security number, they are not speaking about your application/financial aid specifically; they are just giving you general information to get you off the phone.

Two weeks after you have submitted your application to a college, call the admissions office and specifically say, "I would like to know if my file is complete." It is important that you say these exact words. This is different than asking if they have received your application; your application is only one component of your admissions file.

Financial Aid

If you don't receive your Student Aid Report within a few weeks of filing your FAFSA, there is a problem. Call the FAFSA hotline immediately.

Presenting Yourself as a Candidate

Writing Your College Essays

First off, let's distinguish between two very different but equally important college essays: the personal essay and college reflection essays. Your personal essay presents you (the candidate) to the admissions readers. This essay is all about communicating who you are, your personality, your style, your voice as a writer, your unique experiences etc. A college reflection essay communicates how this specific school will benefit and challenge you, and how you can contribute to this specific school community. You may find a school that combines these essays into one. For our purposes, we will approach them as two different essays, although you should be able to weave them together if necessary. The college reflection essay is pretty straightforward. Below you will find some short and simple advice on crafting a college reflection essay. However, crafting a personal essay can be a much more daunting task, and so that section will be presented with much more depth.

College Reflection Essay

You can craft a barebones college reflection essay by using the formula below. Just remember the individual school resources and organizations need to be specific to each individual school. This means you will need to visit campus or do your research online. PLEASE make sure you change the school's name in each college reflection essay.

Paragraphs

Paragraph 1—Talk about what kind of environment you would flourish in as a student and a person. Make sure this environment matches the school you are applying to (small liberal arts, large research university, historically black college, religious institution, etc.).

Paragraph 2—Talk about how attending this particular college will help advance your future goals as a student. This can relate to particular majors you are interested in, study abroad opportunities, research assistantships, etc.

Paragraph 3—Talk about what you have to offer the college/university community. Talk about your interest in participating in certain clubs, working with particular research organizations, or learning from certain professors.

Paragraph 4—Talk about anything they have asked for specifically that isn't already covered, and sum it up.

Feel free to combine these paragraphs or expand upon them as you see fit. Make sure you stay under the word count/character count.

Personal Statement

Here are a few rules to remember when approaching your personal statement.

- This is not an epic novel or autobiography. Therefore, you will select ONE moment or experience to write about. Just one—that's it.
- You should share a memory of something that reveals your personal strengths, or a way in which you grew (personally or academically).
- It's okay to share something personal—just remember this is not a sob story contest. This is a college admission's essay. So, if you choose to share a moment of trauma or difficulty, make sure it clearly communicates some kind of lesson or personal growth.

- Describe, don't tell. Meaning, choose language that puts the reader in your place, as if it were happening right now. Your essay should start like the frame of a movie. Make us feel the textures, sounds, temperature, etc. Don't tell me that it was warm, describe what warmth feels like.
- Start small and work your way out. Start with a single item, a single sound, a single thought. Present this one item in detail, and then zoom out to your surroundings or events.
- Play with time. Slow…things…down. An entire admissions essay could be written about ten seconds of your life: what happened, what you were thinking, the future implications, uncertainties, fears, etc. Or, it could be a series of repeated events: the first day of school for the last fourteen years.

The most powerful personal statement I've read was about shoes. A student of mine wrote about how his apartment had been broken into, and his sneaker collection had been stolen. It opened with him standing in broken glass looking down at the floor where his shoes should have been. He then described the role that these shoes had played in his life, the significance they had for him as a young man in poverty, the status that they granted him, and the hope that he had placed in that status. In those two pages, he was able to present himself as a person, while bringing light to a larger social issue without ever speaking of it directly. Brilliant.

Crafting a good personal essay is going to take time and more help than I can provide you in this section. However, you can definitely use the exercises below to find your personal voice and help you craft a rough draft. Once you have your rough draft, you should seek out the advice of an English teacher or other individual who has a strong command of grammar, punctuation, and writing style.

Brainstorming Exercise

Write a paragraph (minimum) to a page (maximum) for each brainstorming topic. Don't worry about your writing style/grammar/punctuation. This is a brainstorming exercise to help you to connect to potential topics.

For each of the following topics consider:
- What sights, smells, sounds, and emotions come to mind when thinking about this topic?
- What adjectives describe these sights, smells, sounds, and emotions?
- Describe a memory you have of this topic.

An article of clothing that represents you.

A family gathering or tradition.

Describe a moment when you were proud.

Describe a time when you were curious.

Describe a moment when you felt defeated.

Describe the greatest challenge you have faced.

Describe your greatest achievement.

Describe your greatest failure.

Describe your greatest loss.

Describe your greatest win.

Using the brainstorming ideas above, describe one moment in time when you realized something of significance about yourself or the world around you. Be as descriptive as possible. Let the reader feel, hear, and smell the memory. It can be helpful to imagine the moment in slow motion or frozen in time (about one page).

Critiquing Your Essay

Identify the strengths and areas of improvement for your personal essay.

- **Developing Personal Voice**—If your essay does the following, you are on the right track to developing a personal voice. You don't need to have all three, but two of the three would be good.
    - Use anecdotes/ thoughts/ observations unique to you
    - Use strong verbs (*his face growled in disapproval*) instead of adjectives (*he looked at me disapprovingly*).
    - Use metaphor
- **Positive Themes**—The categories below represent common, positive characteristics you might want to demonstrate in your personal essays. If your essay is focused around one of these, you are on the right track. Of course, there are plenty of other positive characteristics and themes, and it is okay if yours is not on this list. Just be sure you can articulate it clearly to whoever is providing you feedback for your essay.

    Does your essay demonstrate:
    1. Your wit and humor
    2. The value of diversity
    3. Your embrace of learning
    4. That you notice the little things/are observant
    5. That you have overcome adversity
    6. A deep commitment to an activity or idea
    7. Your initiative

- **Negative Themes**—The categories below represent common, negative characteristics. These should be identified and removed from your essay, as they may present you in a negative light to the admissions committee.

Does your essay present you as:
1. A cynical person
2. Someone who sees themselves as perfect, or someone who already has life figured out
3. Someone who is likely to be withdrawn in college
4. Depressed
5. Self-destructive
6. Someone with a lack of integrity
7. Someone who blames others

- **Style Test**
  1. Does the essay describe my thoughts and observations (positive), or tell a sequence of events (negative)?
  2. What is my ONE focus/main idea?
  3. Do I go off track anywhere? If so, where?
- **Goals For Your Rewrite**
  1. Articulate the topic
  2. Identify unique perspective
  3. Include positive themes
  4. Remove/avoid negative themes

Once you have rewritten your rough draft and checked the grammar and punctuation over thoroughly, you should pass it off to several other adults for feedback. The key is to write, and rewrite, and rewrite. A crappy first draft is significantly better than no draft at all. You can improve a crappy essay; you can't improve an essay that has yet to be written.

Asking for a Letter of Recommendation

You should plan on needing two to three letters of recommendation. At least one should be from an academic teacher, and the other can be from a principal, counselor, advisor, elective teacher, or sports coach if needed. You must find two teachers/staff who agree to write the letter of recommendation. You will need to provide them with your COMPLETED recommendation request form. DO NOT

WAIT until November or December of your senior year to ask for a recommendation. Teachers are very busy and have a limited amount of time to write letters. If you want a good quality letter, you need to leave them plenty of time.

What do I need to do?

Just approach a teacher with whom you have a good relationship, and ask them to write you a letter of recommendation. You should have already completed the recommendation request form. Having the form filled out ahead of time helps the teacher remember your performance and personality. If they agree, let them know they can keep the form as a reminder slip.

When trying to decide which teacher to approach, ask yourself these questions:
- Which academic classes did I enjoy the most?
- Did I perform well in these classes?
- Did I put forth my best effort in these classes?
- Did I treat my teacher with respect and behave respectfully in these classes?

Frequently Asked Questions

What if I didn't earn the best grade in the class, but I really loved it and put in a lot of effort? If you enjoyed the class and put in a good amount of effort, then you can still consider approaching this teacher—even if your grade was not so hot. However, if you received a D both semesters, you did not really show much improvement, so I would say skip that one.

What if I got an A both semesters, but didn't really get along with the teacher? If you have ever muttered the words, "they just don't like me" about this teacher, or had a difficult time getting along with a teacher, then you should consider asking another teacher. Unless, of course, you have been able to redeem yourself with this teacher since then.

What if I have been a terrible student in my academic classes? If you do not have a single math/science/english class that you have earned a B or better in, then you really have got yourself in a pickle. It is not hopeless though. Think about the electives you have taken and sports that you have played. Yes, an academic teacher would be best, BUT it is more helpful to have a positive recommendation from your music teacher than a negative recommendation from your math teacher.

Request Form

If your college has a specific form for recommendations, make sure you provide it to your recommender. If they do not, go ahead and use the form provided below. If your school uses Naviance, a template will be provided to the teacher when you add them as a recommender in Naviance.

You can copy this page, type up, or handwrite a letter of request form. Either way, it should have the following information on it.

Letter of Recommendation Request Form

Your name

Teacher's name

Date you need the recommendation by

Class(es) you have taken with this instructor

Your grades in those classes

Notes:
    Include a note about one of the following: your proudest academic achievement/contribution that you made in the above class, your favorite project/assignment from this class, or your fondest/best memory you have for the above mentioned class.

College Fair Card Template

Your full name:

Your date of birth:

Your email:

Your address (if you'd like to get mail):

Your phone number:

Your high school:

Your GPA:

Your SAT/ACT:

AP, Honors, or Advanced courses:

Extracurricular Activities:

Special Interests:

Practice Pitches for College Fairs

The following pitches might feel a little awkward at first, but soon they will be rolling off your tongue.

Hello. My name is ____, and I am currently a (freshman/sophomore/junior/senior) at _____ High School. I am interested in possibly pursuing a career in _____ or ____, and I would love to learn more about your school. What are you looking for in a potential candidate?

Hello. My name is ____, and I am currently a (freshman/sophomore/junior/senior) at _____ High School. This summer I had the opportunity to _____, and was wondering if you have any similar opportunities on campus?

Hello. My name is ____, and I am currently a (freshman/sophomore/junior/senior) at _____ High School. I know every college has a unique personality. What do you think is unique about your school?

Hello. My name is ____, and I am currently a (freshman/sophomore/junior/senior) at _____ High School. Some of my favorite courses in high school have been _____ and _____. Can you tell me what the most popular majors are at your school?

Colleges that Offer Fly-Out Programs

Amherst College	Lehigh University
Barnard College	Lewis and Clark College
Bowdoin College	Massachusetts Institute of Technology
Brandeis University	
Bucknell College	Middlebury College
Carleton College	Mount Holyoke College
Colby College	Oberlin College
Colorado College	Occidental College
Connecticut College	Ohio University
Dartmouth College	Pitzer College
Davidson College	Pomona College
Franklin and Marshall	Reed College
George Washington University	Scripps College
Grinnell College	Smith College
Hamilton College	Swarthmore College
Harvey Mudd College	Trinity College
Haverford College	University of Rochester
Holy Cross College	Vermont College
Hope College	Wellesley College
Illinois Wesleyan University	Wesleyan University
Johns Hopkins University	Whitman College
Kalamazoo College	Williams College
Kenyon College	Worcester Polytechnic
Lafayette College	Yale University

Paying for College

The Financial Aid Process

College is expensive; however, all colleges have money set aside to assist students financially. Most colleges offer some assortment of academic scholarships, diversity scholarships, need-based financial aid, and scholarships for students with special talents. However, every college differs in how they support students financially and how much aid they offer. Some colleges offer a lot of aid to low-income students, and some offer almost no aid at all. Oftentimes, prestigious schools have more money to offer in need-based financial aid, although it is more difficult to get accepted at a prestigious college. Public universities, while they have the lowest cost of attendance, usually offer very little in the way of scholarships. How much you pay depends on three main things: your family income, your achievements, and the cost of attendance for your particular college.

In order to get state or federal aid for college you must submit a Free Application for Federal Student Aid (FAFSA). This application is FREE at fafsa.ed.gov. Never pay to file your FAFSA. You should submit your FAFSA online as soon as you can after October 1st. Filing a FAFSA can be a little frustrating, but it is important to remember that the federal government wants to make sure that only students who need money for college get it. So, they have to ask some questions that might feel uncomfortable. But, it's totally worth feeling uncomfortable if it means you get the financial help you need for college. Below is a rundown of what you need to know and do to get your financial aid assistance.

The Financial Aid Checklist for Senior Year

SEPTEMBER
1. Go to https://studentaid.ed.gov/sa/fafsa and watch the YouTube video series on applying for federal student aid: (1) FAFSA Overview, (2) Types of Federal Student Aid, and (3) After You Have Completed The FAFSA.
2. Gather important information. **If you are independent, gather** your social security number, your legal name, your birthdate, and a rough estimate of what you earned this year. If you are married, gather the same information for your spouse. **If you are dependent, gather** your social security number, your legal name, your birthdate, an estimate (rough estimate) of what you earned this year, your parent(s) social security number(s), their exact birthdate(s) including year(s), and a rough estimate of what they earned this year.
3. Determine if you need to file a CSS Profile. Visit http://css-profile.com/schools-require-css-profile/ to determine if any of the schools you are applying to require the CSS profile. The CSS profile is a financial application some schools require, in addition to the FAFSA, to determine your financial aid. If any of your schools are on this list, contact them directly and ask when their CSS profile deadline is.

OCTOBER
4. Create FAFSA IDs for you and your parent(s).
5. File your FAFSA (each college you apply to will need to be added to your FAFSA).
6. Download your Student Aid Report (SAR will be emailed to you) and check for errors. Correct if needed.

JANUARY / FEBRUARY
  6. Link your FAFSA to current taxes.
  7. Submit forms to schools that request it.

MARCH/APRIL
  8. Review your financial aid award letter (March/April).

The only way to know if a certain school is affordable is to get your financial aid award letter and calculate how much you will need to pay. Yes, colleges have a price tag, but rarely do students get stuck with paying the entire bill. Just like buying a car, you can expect that there will be certain discounts that will reduce the sticker price significantly. Scholarships and grants are those discounts. But, it would not be wise to make a decision based solely on that one discount. Why? The fine print. Is the scholarship being offered for one year or four years? Is there a certain GPA requirement to keep the scholarship? Sometimes the school may offer you more money if you communicate to them that you are seriously considering them as a top choice. The only way to know how much out of pocket you are expected to pay is to get a financial aid award letter from the school.

You might not get any additional funding, but many times (especially if your family doesn't have a lot of money) you can get more funding in the award letter than in your acceptance letter. To get an award letter you will need to complete your FAFSA online. The school will then put together your award letter sometime in the spring. Look it over. How much in loans are they proposing you take out? Are there any PLUS loans on the award letter? PLUS are parent loans and should be avoided if you can help it. It's great to have help from your parents—you just want to make sure everyone knows how much this will be total *over four years*. Remember, an award letter tells you how much it will cost for you to attend one year of school (not all four), and often costs go up, and aid goes down every year afterwards. Don't be afraid to ask questions. Money conversations are uncomfortable, but they have to be had. If not, you might be stuck with a bill you can't pay, and end up coming home after your first semester or your first year. Let me tell you, moving back in with your parents is not fun.

Paying for College (Non-US Citizens)

Most undocumented students DO NOT file a FAFSA (even if you have a social security number assigned to you under DACA). If you are not a US citizen or permanent resident, your main source of funding will most likely be private scholarships. Scholarships that are offered to you on your admissions letter are usually NOT need-based and do not require you to file a FAFSA. In addition to scholarships offered to you on your admissions letter, you can pursue private scholarships. All students, regardless of ethnicity or race, can seek out scholarships that do not require citizenship at the Hispanic Scholarship Fund (www.hsf.net) or on Fastweb (www.fastweb.com).

Even without federal aid, there are affordable options for undocumented students depending on where you live. The following states offer undocumented students in-state tuition at public colleges and universities **and** offer state financial aid to assist with the cost of tuition:

- California
- Minnesota
- New Mexico
- Oregon
- Texas
- Washington

NOTE: If you reside in one of the states above, speak to your school counselor about whether you are supposed to file a FAFSA to receive state aid. If you do file, you will still indicate that you are **not** a US Citizen.

If you live in one of the states below, you are eligible to receive in-state tuition at public colleges and universities. If you receive a bill that does not reflect in-state tuition, do not panic. Not all employees at public colleges and universities are familiar with laws regarding tuition for undocumented residents. You will need to call the bursar's office and explain that you are an in-state student graduating from an in-state high school and are eligible for in-state tuition.

- Colorado
- Connecticut
- Florida
- Illinois
- Kansas
- Maryland
- Nebraska
- New Jersey
- New York
- Oklahoma
- Rhode Island
- Utah

In addition to the public colleges and universities above, there are a growing number of private colleges and universities who offer funding for undocumented students.

- Bard College (NY)
- Brown (RI)
- Columbia (NY)
- Cornell (NY)
- Dartmouth (NH)
- Davidson College (NC)
- Dominican University (IL)
- Franklin and Marshall (PA)
- George Mason University (VA)
- Georgetown (DC)
- Harvard (MA)
- Holy Cross College (IN)
- Kenyon College (OH)
- Loyola University Chicago (IL)

- Miami University of Ohio (OH)
- St. Joseph's University (PA)
- Stanford (CA)
- University of Chicago (IL)
- University of Notre Dame (IL)
- Wabash College (IN)
- Williams College (MA)
- Yale (CT)

In addition to the colleges listed above, GetMeToCollege offers a comprehensive list of individual college's policies towards undocumented students. Go to getmetocollege.com. Select the "For Undocumented Students" tab under the "$$ For College" drop-down menu.

If you have read the above resources and cannot find information regarding a particular college, you will need to speak to someone at the college directly. Some colleges also offer need-based scholarships to non US-citizens, but may not openly disclose this. Ask a financial aid counselor at the school if they offer need-based scholarships for undocumented students. If you do not find the individual with whom you are speaking to be knowledgeable or helpful, reach out to someone in the college's Latino resource center or multicultural center to see if they can connect you with a more knowledgeable individual on campus.

Tuition Deposit Plan

Most likely you will need to put down a tuition deposit in order to officially accept admissions at the college or university you have chosen. Tuition deposits can range anywhere from $100 to $600 depending on the school. Some schools require a housing deposit at the same time, and some do not. Remember, in order to reserve your place at the school you will need to accept admissions by whatever date the college has set (usually May 1st). This means you will need a way to pay the deposit before May 1st. I strongly suggest you plan on paying the deposit yourself, unless your parents have agreed to pay it, and have the means to pay it.

Below you will find some questions to keep you on track with saving money for your tuition deposit. Fill it out and be open and honest with the adults in your life who may be able to help you pay the deposit.

1. What is your most expensive tuition deposit?

2. How much money do you have saved as of right now?

3. How much more do you need to save?

4. Do you have a job?

5. What's your plan for raising the tuition deposit?

If you are struggling to save your tuition deposit, call the school before May 1st. Many schools will work with you regarding your tuition deposit, especially if you come from a low-income family.

Applying

Once you start applying you will need two main trackers to keep your college applications in order. Once you start applying use the password sheet for every single college you apply to. If you want to you can also use this for your FAFSA information as well. This form should NEVER leave home unless you are completing applications in class. If so, be sure to stay organized. You do not want to lose these forms! Lastly, as you complete applications, fill in the application tracker. This is a must-do if you want to ensure that you actually receive a decision back from the college! Applications get lost in the shuffle all the time. Your application tracker allows you some peace of mind to know that all is as well.

Password Sheet

ACT/SAT
Website: _____
Your high school ACT/SAT school code: _____
Username: _____
Password: _____
Email you used to sign up: _____

FAFSA
Email you used to sign up: _____
Password: _____
FSAID: _____

Professional/ Appropriate Email
Email: _____
Password: _____

Common Application
Username: _____
Password: _____
Website: _____

College 1
Username: _____
Password: _____
Website: _____

College 2
Username: _____
Password: _____
Website: _____

College 3
Username: _____
Password: _____
Website: _____

College 4
Username: _____
Password: _____
Website: _____

College 5
Username: _____
Password: _____
Website: _____

College 6
Username: _____
Password: _____
Website: _____

College 7
Username: _____
Password: _____
Website: _____

College 8
Username: _____
Password: _____
Website: _____

College 9
Username: _____
Password: _____
Website: _____

College Application Tracker

Follow these steps to ensure you get an admissions decision from every college you apply to. Make sure you complete the tracker as you go.

1. As soon as you submit your application, fill in the college name and admission's phone number into your tracker.
2. Fill in the date you submitted your application and whether you submitted it online or via regular mail.
3. Ask your counselor to send your transcripts. Once they are sent, fill in the date they were sent.
4. About two weeks after you apply, call the admissions office and ask them, "Is my file complete?" If you are missing any items, they will tell you. Make a note of it in the "File missing" box so you can take care of these issues A.S.A.P.

College	Date application sent	Date you spoke to admissions to check file	File missing
Admisions phone number	Date transcripts sent	Is application file complete? (Y/N)	

College	Date application sent	Date you spoke to admissions to check file	File missing
Admisions phone number	Date transcripts sent	Is application file complete? (Y/N)	
College	Date application sent	Date you spoke to admissions to check file	File missing
Admisions phone number	Date transcripts sent	Is application file complete? (Y/N)	
College	Date application sent	Date you spoke to admissions to check file	File missing
Admisions phone number	Date transcripts sent	Is application file complete? (Y/N)	

College	Date application sent	Date you spoke to admissions to check file	File missing
Admisions phone number	Date transcripts sent	Is application file complete? (Y/N)	

College	Date application sent	Date you spoke to admissions to check file	File missing
Admisions phone number	Date transcripts sent	Is application file complete? (Y/N)	

College	Date application sent	Date you spoke to admissions to check file	File missing
Admisions phone number	Date transcripts sent	Is application file complete? (Y/N)	

Decision Time

Once you have completed your applications it is time to compare your student award letters and make a decision! In this section you will find advice on how to interpret your financial aid and a matriculation checklist that will help you stay on top of all the forms and deadlines involved with securing your place in college for the fall.

Interpreting Award Letters

When you first receive your award letter don't expect a perfect financial fit. Sometimes you might luck out and the school might offer you exactly what you need to make it work with help from a relative or a summer job. Most likely, though, you will be a little shy of your goal. And by shy, I mean several thousands shy. You shouldn't panic right away. Schools rarely hand out golden tickets of all expenses paid. Schools only have a certain amount of money to offer potential students, and admissions reps have to be selective about who they extend scholarships to. If a particular school is your top choice, make sure you are communicating that to them. Go to campus. Attend visit days. Speak with the admissions rep early in your college application process, and stay in contact with them up until the day you get that award letter. If you develop a personal connection, and demonstrate your investment in attending a school, the admissions reps might just go the extra mile for you.

Once you get your award letter, sit down and do the math (see below). Calculate how much you need total (tuition+ fees+ room+ meal plan+ about $1000 for books), and how much aid you are being offered (grants+ scholarships+ unsubsidized loans+ subsidized loans+ Perkins loans). **Do not include PLUS loans in this calculation.** PLUS loans are not guaranteed. They rely on your parent's credit score, and your parent(s) will have to apply for and be approved for a new loan every year. PLUS loans put your financial future in a precarious position because you can't predict the future. What if your parent loses a job? What if their financial circumstances change? Instead, ask your parents directly how much they can contribute annually to your college expenses. It is important that they give you an actual number. If they can't give you a number, then chances are they have the best intentions to help you out, but might not actually be able to come through when you get the bill. You will also need to ask them whether you will be covered under their insurance policy in college. If so, you will need to submit proof of such or you will be charged extra for health insurance. Once you have calculated how much your total costs are, and how much aid you are getting, subtract the two. If your parents have given you a number for how much they can contribute annually, go ahead and subtract that too. This final amount is how much you will need to come up with *in cash* every year to attend. Know this number. Write it down. Circle it. Because this is the number you are going to have to communicate to the admissions rep when discussing additional aid.

Comparing Your Options

College name	Graduation rate
YOUR AID	**YOUR COSTS**
Grants $_____	Tuition $_____
Scholarships $_____	Housing $_____
Subsidized loans $_____	Meal plan $_____
Unsub. loans $_____	Fees $_____
Perkins loans $_____	Books $_____
TOTAL AID $_____	TOTAL AID $_____
Total Aid − Total Costs	= Cash Out of Pocket
_____ _____	_____

College name		Graduation rate	
YOUR AID		**YOUR COSTS**	
Grants	$_____	Tuition	$_____
Scholarships	$_____	Housing	$_____
Subsidized loans	$_____	Meal plan	$_____
Unsub. loans	$_____	Fees	$_____
Perkins loans	$_____	Books	$_____
TOTAL AID	$_____	TOTAL AID	$_____
Total Aid − Total Costs = Cash Out of Pocket _____ _____ _____			

College name		Graduation rate	
YOUR AID		**YOUR COSTS**	
Grants	$_____	Tuition	$_____
Scholarships	$_____	Housing	$_____
Subsidized loans	$_____	Meal plan	$_____
Unsub. loans	$_____	Fees	$_____
Perkins loans	$_____	Books	$_____
TOTAL AID	$_____	TOTAL AID	$_____
Total Aid − Total Costs = Cash Out of Pocket _____ _____ _____			

College name	Graduation rate
YOUR AID	**YOUR COSTS**
Grants $_____	Tuition $_____
Scholarships $_____	Housing $_____
Subsidized loans $_____	Meal plan $_____
Unsub. loans $_____	Fees $_____
Perkins loans $_____	Books $_____
TOTAL AID $_____	TOTAL AID $_____

Total Aid − Total Costs = Cash Out of Pocket

_____   _____   _____

College name	Graduation rate
YOUR AID	**YOUR COSTS**
Grants $_____	Tuition $_____
Scholarships $_____	Housing $_____
Subsidized loans $_____	Meal plan $_____
Unsub. loans $_____	Fees $_____
Perkins loans $_____	Books $_____
TOTAL AID $_____	TOTAL AID $_____

Total Aid − Total Costs = Cash Out of Pocket

_____   _____   _____

College name		Graduation rate	
YOUR AID		**YOUR COSTS**	
Grants	$_____	Tuition	$_____
Scholarships	$_____	Housing	$_____
Subsidized loans	$_____	Meal plan	$_____
Unsub. loans	$_____	Fees	$_____
Perkins loans	$_____	Books	$_____
TOTAL AID	$_____	TOTAL AID	$_____
Total Aid − Total Costs = Cash Out of Pocket			
_____ _____ _____			

Good thing you took the time to develop that chummy rapport with the admissions rep, because now you are going to need it. By now you should have already visited your top choice schools to show how serious you are about attending college there. If this is the case, then discussing additional aid should be something you can do over the phone. If the schools you are considering are local, make sure you take the time to go in and discuss additional funding with the rep in person. Be specific. Tell the rep that you are eager to accept admissions, but need $_____ additional aid to be able to attend. The conversation might be a little confusing, especially if the rep is thinking through different possibilities out loud. If the rep has indicated that they can offer additional funding, make sure you are clear whether these additional funds will be grants (yes!), scholarships (yes!), or loans (wait a minute). Update your financial aid calculator with the new amounts and make sure you are comfortable with your total in loans and out of pocket.

Sometimes, there is not enough creative math in the world to make attending your dream college possible. This is the heartbreaker of all heartbreakers. Knowing when to walk away from your dream school is going to require that you put on that adult hat you have now earned, tip it kindly, put one foot in front of the other, and focus on walking into the future you can have.

College Matriculation Checklist

Admission's Phone: _____

Financial Aid: _____

By May 1st

This is the BIG day! Be sure to submit your intent to enroll and your tuition deposit by the deadline (traditionally May 1st).

Submit intent to enroll—You do this usually online through the college's web portal. There will be a box you will have to check to indicate to the school that you are accepting their admission's offer.

Tuition deposit—The intent to enroll and the tuition deposit usually go hand in hand. Your tuition deposit is the ONLY way you can be sure to reserve your seat for the fall. When you accept admissions you usually have to pay your tuition deposit at that time, either online with a credit card or by check via mail.

Housing deposit—The housing deposit is similar to the tuition deposit. If you will be living on campus you will need to submit your deposit for the dorms. This is sometimes due May 1st and sometimes later. If you can't afford the housing deposit and the tuition deposit at the same time, the tuition deposit is your priority.

Accept financial aid offer—You will need to accept the financial aid you have been awarded, even the grants and scholarships. Log-on to your college portal and check out the financial aid tab. If you are confused at all, call the financial aid office and ask them what you need to do to finalize your award.

Complete loan entrance counseling—Similar to your master promissory note, you will also need to complete loan entrance counseling if you are taking any student loans. This can be done online at studentloans.gov.

Submit your master promissory note—One of the things you will need to do before the school can distribute your financial aid loans is complete a master promissory note. This can be done online at studentloans.gov.

By June 1st

Register for orientation—Registering for orientation can be easy or ridiculously difficult, depending on what college you attend. Keep an eye out for an email about orientation. If you haven't heard by June 15th, call the school and get signed up.

Schedule academic advising meeting—Most schools assign advisors to students; however, some schools do not. Likewise, most schools require advisors to meet with their students at least once before the first semester; however, some have advising on a first-come, first-serve basis with no scheduled meetings. Look online or call the admissions office to find out when you will meet with your academic advisor for the first time. You will most likely have some kind of initial advising meeting as part of your orientation schedule.

Submit vaccination documents: Before you can attend class (or sometimes even register) you will need to submit your vaccination records to the school. Your high school may have a copy of these on file, but don't count on it. Ask well in advance, so you have time to get a copy of the records from your physician. If you cannot locate a copy of your vaccination records, you may need to get specific vaccinations again to satisfy this requirement.

Immediately After Graduation

Order official final transcripts from your high school to be sent to your college.

CPSIA information can be obtained
at www.ICGtesting.com
Printed in the USA
BVHW070013111122
651554BV00005B/308

9 781939 054760